BASIC SPEECH COMMUNICATION

Elin Jeri Schikler
Linda Tamesian Kalfayan

University Press of America, Inc.
Lanham • New York • London

Copyright © 1996 by
University Press of America,® Inc.
4501 Forbes Boulevard, Suite 200
Lanham, Maryland 20706

3 Henrietta Street
London, WC2E 8LU England

Library of Congress Cataloging-in-Publication Data

Schikler, Elin Jeri.
Basic speech communication / Elin Jeri Schikler, Linda Tamesian
Kalfayan.
p.   cm.
Includes bibliographical references.
1. Oral communication. I. Kalfayan, Linda Tamesian. II. Title.
P95.S35   1996   302.2'242--dc20   96-15019 CIP

ISBN 0-7618-0360-2 (pbk: alk. ppr.)
ISBN: 978-0-7618-0360-7

Dedication

Dedicated to the memory of my father
Morton Scheiber
who always ran in as quick as a bunny
whenever I needed him,
and to
my darling husband Jeff, fabulous daughter Ilana,
and perfect mother Nadine

Love forever - Elin

Dedicated to my loving huband
and our newly born first child
Gregory
You are every star in my universe.

Love - Linda

Table of Contents

Chapter 1 **Communication Overview** **1**
"Do I Take Communication for
Granted?"

Chapter 2 **The Self as Communicator** **11**
"Who Am I?"

Chapter 3 **Interpersonal Communication** **21**
"How Well Do We Get Along?"

Chapter 4 **Listening** **33**
"Listen Up, Please"

Chapter 5 **Small Group Communication** **43**
"Am I A Team Player?"

Chapter 6 **The Verbal Message - Language** **49**
"What Did You Mean By That?"

Chapter 7 **Voice and Speech** **57**
"Is How I Uh, Say, What I Say, Um,
Important?"

Chapter 8   **Public Speaking Situations**   69
"Can I Capture the Crowd?"

Chapter 9   **Nonverbal Communication**   79
"Take a Guess...What do I Mean?"

Chapter 10   **Interviewing Skills**   91
"Can I Have This Job Please?"

Chapter 11   **Large Group Dynamics**   107
"Am I An Effective Communicator?"

Bibliography   113

Acknowledgments

I would like to thank many important people in my life and career who have inspired me to learn, to teach, and to nurture.

I thank Edward and Ann Tamesian - my parents - for their pursuit in giving me a sound and reflective education. I thank the worldly education of my uncles and aunts who have taught me that education is a tool for survival. I thank my sister Joyce, who introduced me to the wonderful world of speech communication. To Simone, Jason, and Dr. John...I thank you for all of your special hugs.
To my mentors, Dr. Ann Seidler, Doris Bianchi, and Dr. Wayne Bond - Thank you for all of your teachings. To my friends, who are always there for me either at the end of the telephone line, or at arms distance...I thank you for your counsel.

I thank you all for working with me yesterday for today, and today for all the tomorrows.

Linda

I would like to thank a number of people who helped create a peaceful and helpful atmosphere for the writing of this book.

First - my husband Jeff, who kept smiling (and napping) regardless of my mood swings; my daughter Ilana, who kept dancing and singing through it all; my mother, who always had a kind, reassuring word to remind me that I could do this; my sister Elise, who said that she knew I could do something aside from singing; my father, who was beside me in spirit every step of the way; and Inga, my sweet Cracker Jack prize who has been with my family for 38 years - and sat by my side every day.

I would also like to thank Dr. Philip Dolce, Dean of the Social Science-Communication Arts Department at Bergen Community College for his guidance, support, and belief in this project.

Elin

Preface

This book is designed to help the student in a basic speech communication class with an emphasis on practice skills in speaking, listening, and presentational skills. Although a foundational approach has been taken here, the instructor is free to utilize the contents in its entirety, or as a platform to build upon depending on their specific needs and areas of expertise.

The book covers listening skills, presentational skills, interpersonal communication, public speaking, voice and speech improvement, nonverbal communication, group discussion, and interviewing skills. Many of the chapters have exercises that can be done as in-class activities, or as homework assignments. They are set up in such a way as to allow students the freedom to create, or add to, the ideas presented.

We realize that in some schools, students are not required to learn the theory and practice of standard American English. Our chapter on this topic may be used as a purely theoretical resource, or it can simply be geared to the needs of the individual student.

It has been our experience that a basic course in speech communication is a strong subject to build upon in terms of helping students in other areas of study: learning to listen more effectively, and presenting thoughts in a clear and precise fashion are just a few of the effective tools needed in most - if not all - subject areas. The activities in this book, as well as the basic concepts discussed, allow each student the opportunity to be active participants in the crucial area of speech communication skills.

Chapter 1

Communication Overview
"Do I Take Communication For Granted?"

Human Communication begins with our first breath;with our first cry . In the movies, and in reality, we are always shown the newborn baby being slapped on the rear, and from that moment on, he/she is considered to be a viable human being - one capable of sustaining life on its own. But is this statement true? Can we truly sustain life "on our own?". On a physical level, possibly; but on a mental and emotional level, probably not. We need other people to survive. Everywhere we go, and everything we do is in some measure dependent upon other people. In other words, we do not, and cannot, live in a vacuum.

If we were to sit down and write just a few of the words that come to mind when we think of human communication, the following would probably head the list:

feelings	past experiences
television	beliefs
facial expressions	listening
body language	messages
sign language	newspapers
music	gaining knowledge
emotions	telephone
attitudes	sharing
magazines	taking polls
speaking	reading
music	writing
computer	arguments

When two or more people get together, there is communication. Even if there is not a single word spoken, there is still communication. Let us understand then, right from the outset, that there is no such thing as *no* communication- it is a constant in our lives. As we will see in a later chapter, there is communication even when other people are not involved. (Intrapersonal). It is important to understand that the entire communication process involves messages. These messages are sent and received through the use of symbols (which may be gestures), and language.

Human communication situations involving symbols

1. You walk to a bus stop and there are two people sitting on the bench waiting. You patiently stand by the side of that bench. Without a word spoken, a message is sent to the other people who respond by moving over to allow room for you to sit.
2. You are standing in a very crowded room, and someone is moving quickly through the crowd. Without a word, without your questioning what the problem might be, you wordlessly move aside to let the person pass.

Exercise

Divide yourselves into groups of three or four people. Think of four other communication situations where symbols are used to allow for a message to be sent.

Verbal Language

We send many of our messages through the use of language. Language is the spoken word, but is it something that we take for granted? Think about the following statement: "When I speak, you listen, and understand what I'm saying." Ultimately, this would be a great achievement, but there are times when the spoken word is misunderstood - even if we speak the same language. As an example, if I mention long, red, shiny hair, the image that may pop up in your mind might be that of Cindy Lauper, Lucille Ball, or even Ronald McDonald. Yet in my mind, I may have actually been thinking, and talking, about the coat of hair on an Irish Setter. The point here is that words mean different things to different people; they conjure up different images. Let's examine the following statements in terms of your particular meaning, and we will see how each person in your group either agrees , or differs, with your chosen interpretation.

What is:
1. The name given to the night before Halloween.
2. The name given to a very large truck.
3. The name given to the summer bug that lights up.
4. The name given to a large sandwich ordered at a deli.
5. The name given to a tourist.
6. The name given to the topping on an ice cream cone.
7. The name given to the body of water near your house.
8. The name given to the steps outside a house.
9. The name given to a very large bee.
10. The name given to the item that a child uses to fill sand with at the beach.

<u>Exercise</u>

Discuss other words, or statements, that may have more than one interpretation. An example of a word that may have more than one meaning is BAD. This may mean terrible, rotten, great, or cool.

Nonverbal transmission of messages

Messages may be sent and received through nonverbal cues. When we speak of nonverbal messages, we are talking about our movement, posture, gestures, facial expressions, and the tone of our voice.(paralanguage) Nonverbal communication aids verbal messages in that it strengthens the ideas that are being sent, as well as helping to clearly pinpoint the meaning. As an example, if I were standing on the street with my arms folded across my chest, this may indicate a number of possible meanings: 1. I'm chilly. 2. I am annoyed about what someone is saying to me. 3. I'm angry. 4. I'm embarrassed. Without the spoken word, it is obvious that the message being sent may not necessarily be received correctly. Think about the following questions:
1. When someone says hello to you without a smile, what is the message being sent, and what is the message being received?
2. When someone says they'll get together with you, but it never happens, what's really going on?
3. When a person says "thank you" using a very low pitched,

slowly paced voice, what are they really saying?

<u>Exercise</u>

Try to formulate your own situations where a person says one thing verbally, and another nonverbally. Which one do you believe?

The Communication Process

Communication is a circular process. This is due to the fact that it is both a dynamic process, and one that has more than one step. Let us assume that you raise your hand in class to answer a question (you're now sending a message). The teacher sees your hand up, but calls on someone else (she received the message). There is more going on here however. When the teacher decided not to call on you, she was sending out another message to you. What that actual message was can be left to anyone's individual interpretation. In other words, there is a sender and a receiver in the communication process, but the sender is also a receiver and vice versa. The sender is also known as the **encoder,** or the **source,** and the receiver as the **decoder.**

Feedback

Feedback is an answer or a response, and can be verbal or nonverbal. The actual term "feedback" has been taken from the academic scope of physical science to explain how a thermostat functions. Let us assume that you set your thermostat to 70. The heated or cooled air will adjust itself so that it reaches that temperature, and will continue to regulate itself to maintain that level of comfort. Similarly, human communication functions on this systematic giving and receiving to get feedback - an answer, subsequent understanding, and level of comfort.

Communication Model

In order to fully understand the communication model, we must think of it in terms of sectors:

<u>Sector 1</u> - Here, the sender (source/encoder) thinks of an idea that they wish to convey. He/she gathers this information from their particular **frame of reference** which is one's past experiences,

knowledge, feelings, emotions, attitudes, and beliefs.

<u>Sector 2</u> - This sector represents the actual message being sent. The message may be expressed verbally, nonverbally, or a combination of both.

<u>Sector 3</u> - In this sector, the receiver (decoder) breaks down the message according to their frame of reference.

<u>Sector 4</u> - Feedback (an answer or a response) is given - either verbally or nonverbally.

<u>Sector 5</u>- We use a **channel,** or a medium, to transmit our messages. This channel is usually our five senses - sight, sound, touch, taste, and smell, but may also fall into the category of electronic and print media.

Communication Situations

There are four basic kinds of communication situations:

1. One-to-one communication
2. Small group communication
3. Public speaking
4. Print Media and Electronic communication.

In each of the communication situations mentioned above, there is a sender, a receiver, a message, and some form of feedback. All of this in an attempt to achieve one major goal - understanding.

<u>Exercise</u>

1. <u>One-to-one communication</u> - Divide into pairs. Take approximately five minutes to interview, and be interviewed, by one another. Take another five minutes to organize your thoughts, and write down some notes. Now, instead of introducing yourself, introduce your partner to the group.

In most cases, when people come into a new class, they feel uneasy. There are many reasons for this, and they vary from person to person. For the most part, however, the uneasiness stems from unfamiliarity with the room, the people, and the situation. It's always difficult telling a group of strangers about yourself because you don't know if they'll like you, or find you boring, or silly, or downright stupid. Very few people enjoy being put in that position. By having a **dyadic** communication experience, (one to-one) the transition becomes less painful, and far less embarrassing.

2. <u>Small group communication</u> - Divide yourself into pairs. Look around the room and decide which other pair you would like to join with. Once you get together (now there are four of you), introduce yourselves. After a few minutes, look around again and choose two more pairs to join you (now there are eight people), and discuss your hobbies (or something else that's not too "deep".) If you don't know the people well, it's always easiest to begin with discussions that are comfortable, and non-threatening.

Once a level of comfort is reached within the group, a problem-solving situation should be considered. Using the **consensus** of the group (a consensus is *all* group members in agreement), rank - in order of importance - which characteristics make a teacher most effective. Number one will represent the most important characteristic, and number ten, the least. Keep in mind that there must be total agreement between the members of your group:

<u>The Effective Teacher</u>

Good speaking voice
Encourages students to think for themselves
Tolerant of individual's problems
Understands the needs of their students
Is very knowledgeable about the subject area
Is warm and friendly
Does not choose favorites
Does not yell, or embarrass anyone
Enforces discipline; has total control of the class
Devotes most class time having group discussions

Once your group has reached its unanimous decision, discuss the following: Do you feel that your group operated effectively? Was the group more concerned with completing the assignment, or with taking their time, and allowing every person to speak? How did your group decide to organize the importance of each characteristic? Was there any one person who seemed to significantly influence the group? Did you feel comfortable expressing your own beliefs?

3. <u>Public speaking</u> - Create a one minute speech to be given in front of the class choosing one of the following areas:

1. Your hobbies, or things you like to do in your spare time.

2. Your favorite foods, or foods that you dislike.
3. Music that you like, or dislike.
4. Places that you have traveled to, or would like to see.
5. Aspects of your life that you find satisfying/not satisfying.
6. Your education, and your feelings about why you're here.
7. Your personal goals for the next five years.
8. Habits you have that you wish you could change.
9. Your most embarrassing moment.

Now create a two to three minute speech on one of the following topics: Remember, now the speech is a little longer, so make sure that your thoughts are clear, and well organized.

1. What do you feel are some of the mistakes that your parents made in terms of raising you? How would you ensure that you would not make the same errors?
2. Discuss some of your wishes/ dreams/ expectations in life.
3. What have you done in your life that you most regret?
4. Discuss the occasions in your life that have made you the happiest.
5. What are your usual ways of dealing with anger, anxiety, and frustration?
6. Who are the people that have significantly helped you in your life? (Name one or two)
7. Your views on why people should get married - or why they should not.
8. What things worry you the most in terms of your life now, and in terms of your future?
9. Discuss someone that you feel you have helped significantly.

After listening to what people had to say, see if you can analyze the different answers. Were the responses similar? If not, in what ways specifically did they differ? Was it easier to speak for a longer period of time?

4. Print Media and Electronic Communication - Assume for the moment that you are a newspaper reporter. Choosing a "topical" subject, write a well developed paragraph clearly illustrating your opinion on the subject. Do you find that the media effects your behavior? Your mood? How does it effect the people around you?

Now consider electronic communication. "Grease" is a record, a cassette, a CD, a play, and a movie. The same story, same humor, same characters, same music...but is it the same? Think of the differences, and how each media form effects you. Are you more moved/excited by the movie, or the show? Do you prefer listening to the music and visualizing your own "drama", rather than having it played out in front of you?

Keep in mind that regardless of your feelings, there are no "right" or "wrong" answers. Different people feel differently about different things based on their upbringing, their family, their friends, their experiences, their beliefs, values, and attitudes. How and why they are effected by the media that surrounds them is determined by these factors.

Barriers in Communication

Barriers in communication will be discussed in a later chapter, but for our purposes here, let it suffice to say that a **barrier** is anything that stops, blocks, or hinders the communication process leading to misunderstandings between people. These barriers arise because of our: 1.Speaking skills; 2. Listening skills; 3.Language skills; 4. Interpersonal skills; 5. Intrapersonal skills; 6. Group communication skills.

Exercise

Arrange your group into a large circle. Whoever decides to go first will state their name, and an obscure profession (try to think of something really unusual).The next person will repeat the name and profession of the first person, and then add their own. This will continue until each person has had a chance to say something. This "game" will become increasingly more difficult as each person speaks since there is more to remember. Once the activity is completed, discuss why some people seemed better than others at remembering the information. Was this strictly a matter of intelligence, or were there other factors involved?

1. **Speaking skills** - How do I sound to others? Too loud; Too soft; Too nasal; Too high; Too slow; Too tense; Too muffled; Do I sound like I care; Am I lacking expression; Do I leave sounds out of words making it difficult to understand what I'm saying; Do I add too many extra sounds to words; Do I speak in a monotone?

2. **Listening skills** - Do I impede the communication process because: I seem uninterested; I daydream; I sit inattentively; I never bother to take notes; I get too emotional; I argue too much; I let noise interfere; Am I more concerned with the way a person looks, or with what they are saying; Am I too easily distracted?

3. **Language skills** - Do I hinder the communication process by: making too many assumptions; not bothering to properly categorize; being unaware of the uniqueness of the language; not understanding, or being able to properly utilize, the structure of the language?

4. **Interpersonal skills** - The message that was sent was not clear based on the fact that I did not have the proper frame of reference for the information. My past experiences, knowledge, feelings, emotions, attitudes, and beliefs, unfortunately got in the way of my understanding what was going on.

5. **Intrapersonal skills** - Due to certain problems within myself, communication was difficult, if not impossible. I was: very hungry; extremely tired; angry; depressed; I had too many other things on my mind; I was not feeling well.

6. **Group Communication Skills** - Communication within the context of a group is always difficult since it is highly improbable that all involved will be in total agreement on any given issue. Each of us is unique. Although there may be many similarities between us, there are as many, if not more, dissimilarities. This is important to remember. We need to evaluate the following questions:

* Am I a team player ?
* Do I care about what's going on ?
* Am I concerned with becoming an integral part of the group ?
* Am I honest ?
* Do I make fair judgments ?
* Do I hear only what I want to hear ?
* Do I acknowledge and care about others' feelings ?

Communicating with other people is something we will spend the rest of our lives doing. This may be a pleasant thought for some of us, and an unnecessary burden for others. We are, and will continue to be, speakers and listeners; participants and observers. We are - each of us - part of a world where good communication skills can determine how successful we will be.

At this time, you are a college student. One of the reasons you are sitting in this class is because it is part of a program that will inevitably lead to your receiving a degree. That degree - regardless of the subject area - will lead to your going out into the world to "make your mark." It is probable that you will meet with, and have dealings with, a great many people along the way. PEOPLE is the operative word here. You will be surrounded by, and working along with, people, for a good portion of your life.

With this in mind, it would make a great deal of sense to ask yourself whether the communication skills you have at present are good enough to ensure a successful future. If you are in the majority of those of us who feel there are some minor glitches to work out, then join the crowd. How you interact with others is crucial. If you believe this statement to be true, then you are well on your way to becoming an effective communicator.

Remember: Good communicators are made, not born. This is not as natural a process as you would like to believe. Hard work, understanding, knowledge, compassion, and good old fashioned common sense, are the keys to success.

Chapter 2

The Self as Communicator
"Who Am I ?"

Intrapersonal Communication is communication within oneself. It is something that begins as soon as you are born, and continues throughout your life. Your parents, siblings, relatives, teachers, friends, and enemies, will ultimately contribute to who you are, and what you think and believe, but much of what goes on in your life is "selected" by you. There are a number of sources from which intrapersonal communication stems from. Examining each will help to understand the entire process.

Self-Esteem is what you think and believe about yourself. It may not have anything to do with what other people think or believe about you, but it has a great deal to do with your overall personality. If you have always felt unattractive, then all the compliments in the world will not help you to truly believe that you may actually be pretty or handsome. Chances are, the nice things that are said about you will simply be thought of as pity or decency. For some reason, once you make up your mind about "who" and "what" you are, those beliefs stick - sometimes for a lifetime. Therefore, your self-esteem may be defined as the attitude, feeling, and impression you have about yourself. These impressions will have a tremendous effect on those around you since you may not ever change your own basic personality. A shy person acts a certain way towards others, and in turn, is treated in a particular way by others. Sometimes, people may feel uncomfortable with each other due to a number of mixed signals. Our shy person may try to become friendly with someone who they have noticed with other people is very open, friendly, and vivacious, only to find that they act very differently towards them. This might make the shy person think that there is something wrong with them, when in actuality, the other person involved may feel foolish acting the way they usually do with such a shy person. Many misunderstandings and insecurities happen between people who simply misread signals.One may ask, "How did you get to be the way you are?" "Why, or what, made you so angry / happy / bitter / obnoxious / shy?"

These questions are very difficult to answer, and lie in the core of our being.The fact that so many intelligent, educated people seek out professional help is testament to the fact that understanding others is very hard, but perhaps not quite as difficult as understanding ourselves. Looking at the sources of self-concept will help clear up some of the answers to who and what and why you are the way you are.

The Physical Image

Nobody is entirely happy with the way they look. Some of us can look in a mirror - with nothing on - and find some measure of satisfaction...although there's always something to complain about. Probably the biggest problem in this area is the inability for many people to accept the fact that they have a particular body "type." An **endomorph** has a genetic predisposition towards being softer and rounder; the **ectomorph** is thin and lean; the **mesomorph** is athletic and muscular. Your body type is determined at the moment of conception, and cannot be escaped - regardless of exercise or diet. Although it is true that you can improve upon your basic frame, certain changes will never take place. A female with short legs may diet and pump iron at the gym - but she will always be short-legged. The actual bone structure does not change.

It is very easy to say that this knowledge should bring an element of comfort to us; that we should more readily be able to accept ourselves the way we are - but it does not seem to work that way. For the most part, we are prisoners of our particular society. The American ideal today is a slender, healthy, slightly tanned, athletic individual. This "ideal" is both calorie conscious, and aware of how many fat grams are consumed in a day. It is apparent that the perception of our bodies is determined, in part, by the acceptable standards of the day. The great masters of their day - Reubens and DaVinci - were noted for their paintings of voluptuous women; ladies, who by today's standards would be considered heavy and out of shape, yet in their day, considered the ideal. In the 1960s, the super model Twiggy had the sought after look; waif-thin, and leggy. Today, some people would say that she was in serious need of a good workout at the gym to get "some definition."

How we actually look, and how we perceive we look to others has a definite effect on how we decide to live our lives. The people who are ashamed of their bodies might be reluctant to participate in certain areas, and may actually feel threatened by others who can become involved in those activities, due to their own insecurities.

Very young children have the right idea here. They are still too young to judge each other on the basis of physical characteristics; they don't judge a person's worth by how muscular, or slender, or tan they are, but rather on whether that person is fun to play with. It's too bad that some of the adults in our society have forgotten this important fact.

Talents

Each of us has a talent for something. Some people are natural athletes, whereas others have musical or artistic abilities. There are people who can cook, and yet others who can actually fix a car. The problem with talent is that if we decide we *don't* have it, we rarely bother to aspire to try anything. On a recent talk show, the actor Chuck Norris was being interviewed. When asked what he attributed his fame to, he responded by telling the audience that he had been raised in a town where the notion of fame was nothing more than a pipe dream. He stated that "It's not how good you are, but how bad you want it."

If each of us could believe this statement, then we would be able to feel more confident about reaching for our goals. In the early sixties, a singing team by the name of The Smothers Brothers was performing in New Jersey. They were not the headliners, but rather the opening act for a comedian. In a case like this, it is not uncommon for the audience to be a little restless waiting for "the star". While Tommy and Dickie Smothers were trying to sing, a few people in the audience began to heckle them. Instead of panicking, the experienced singers played along with the audience and started joking around. Today, those of us who remember them fondly, know them as one of the best comedy teams of the sixties. Unfortunately, their careers came to an end when their popular television program was canceled due to their insistence on joking about political issues.

It is an interesting fact that their brand of humor would easily be accepted in the nineties, but was not considered appropriate thirty years earlier. Once again, we see how our society dictates what is, or what is not, acceptable at a given time.

Experiences

Many experiences that we have in life are self-chosen, but others are imposed upon us. As small children, we may choose to play with certain toys, and totally ignore others. But it is also true that many toys are originally chosen by the adults around us, so are we really making a choice at all? As adults, we are in a better position to increase our choices, thereby increasing our experiences. The more you experience, the more you grow socially and intellectually. This will lead to better intrapersonal communication skills, and ultimately build up your interpersonal skills as well.

Remember - not all experiences are positive. There are things that we do in life that are silly, embarrassing, or not very well thought out. This however is a learning experience in itself. Almost anything that you can learn from is positive. The old saying that some of us "have to learn the hard way" is probably true. There are times when we must experience some things on our own to determine whether we should, or should not, have done them.

Social Roles

Our roles in life vary with the passage of time. You are a son / daughter, a student, a friend, a cousin, a teacher, a husband / wife, a singer, an aunt / uncle, a plumber. Each of these roles are a part of who you are. In a sense, **roles** are different parts that you play in your life. But unlike a role, or part, in a play, these roles are real. They represent who you are at various stages of your life.

Similar to the experiences you have in life, some roles are assigned to you, whereas others are chosen. You do not choose whether you will be a sister or brother - your parents make that choice for you; but you *do* choose whether or not you will be charming and loving to that sister or brother.

Many of the roles we adopt are chosen from models around us. If you are crazy about your father, then you will try to follow in his footsteps. If you feel however that you come from a dysfunctional family, you may choose another one to emulate. If you are attracted to a particular performer - to their style of dress, or personality, you may wish to copy them.

Roles can, and usually do, change. As an eight year old child, you may have been very shy, soft-spoken, and respectful towards your parents; as an eighteen year old, this respect may have turned to rebellion, and possibly animosity; as a twenty eight year old, the relationship may evolve into a comfortable feeling of equality and friendship; and as a thirty eight year old, the roles may reverse altogether, making you a sort of caretaker to your own parents.

The roles that you take on in life -whether voluntarily, or imposed upon you by society - form a basic part of your personality and are therefore crucial to your social value system.

Values, Attitudes, and Beliefs

People have a tendency to use these three words interchangeably as if each meant the same as the other. In truth, they are connected, but vary in scope. These aspects of yourself influence the way you perceive yourself, and the way you perceive everything and everyone around you.

Values are those things that are shared by a large group of people, a country, or a society. They are the things that provide you with the guidelines as to what is right and wrong. Values are usually formed very early in life, and are strongly influenced by family members. If you are raised in a family that values music and education, chances are you will place a high value on those things too. It's almost as if it were part of your basic nature. Unlike the roles you have in life which may change over time, values tend to remain the same throughout your life. If they do change at all - they do so very slowly.

Attitudes are those things that stem from your basic value system. If you are raised believing that education is crucial to your life, there is a good possibility that you will go on to college, and possibly graduate school. In a sense, you might say that those things which you value in life will have an effect on your attitude towards the things that you decide to do in life.

Beliefs stem from both your values and attitudes, but are more numerous than either one. You may value education, and your attitude towards it may pull you in the direction of furthering your course work, yet you may have different beliefs as to which college is better, which campus is more suited to your personality, which courses to take, and which teachers you would best get along with. They may change depending on your age, or the social circle you are traveling in.

Expectations

Expectations are messages you send to yourself concerning those things that you expect / want to happen in the future. If you tell yourself that you are going to be a star on Broadway, you will undoubtedly place a great deal of value on theater, will have a positive attitude towards it, and will believe that you can accomplish your ultimate goal. Having expectations in life are positive goals, and give people something to work for, and look forward to.

Daydreaming comes into play here. Many of us dream about what our future holds for us, and sometimes those dreams will sustain us through difficult periods in our lives. If we feel that there is something decent ahead for us, it's easier to face each day.

A Self-fulfilling prophecy is a situation where you make a prediction about whether something will happen, or not happen, and then *make it come true*. An example of this might be deciding ahead of time that your vacation will be a waste of time and money, and then putting yourself in the frame of mind to have a terrible time. This is actually an easy thing to do by simply focusing on the negative aspects only, rather than on the positive.

If you decide that you are a terrible math student, and are prone to failure, you will not try to succeed in that area because you know that you will continue to fail - regardless of what you do.

It is interesting that the self-fulfilling prophecy can be positive. When a coach gives a pep talk to his team before a game, and tells them that they're the best, and that they're going to win, he may succeed in giving each person the confidence to believe that they *will* win. They believe ahead of time that things will work out to their advantage. In other words, they would have successfully fulfilled the prophecy of success.

Psychological Limitations

We all have what may be called an **Ego Defense Network.** This network protects our self concept, thereby helping us to cope with problems, or protecting our "way of life." There are many interesting, yet disturbing stories regarding children who have been so badly abused that they take on different personalities in order to protect their original "self." They escape the pain, humiliation, and abuse by turning inward, becoming another person. In actuality, it is their only protection.

On a less severe level, all of us protect ourselves from negativity by tuning people out. It is amazing how each of us manages to see and hear only those things that we wish to see or hear. If you think your friend is the perfect human specimen, you may disregard or totally tune out anything negative said about them. You do this to protect your image of them. This may also work in reverse. If you dislike someone intensely, you will tend to listen to, or believe only those things that are negative about them; anything nice will be ignored, disbelieved, or simply "not heard."

The Johari Window

Self-awareness can be examined in many different ways, but perhaps the best is through the **Johari window.** The window is a metaphoric division of the self into four separate, yet independent, aspects of the inner self. The four "panes," or sections are: The *open self, blind self, hidden self,* and *unknown self.*

The **open self** represents all the feelings, beliefs, attitudes, and behaviors that are known to yourself and others. It is the part of you that you don't mind sharing, because they are things that you feel comfortable about. This information might include your religion, political beliefs, ideas on fashion, or taste in music. It may also include your age - depending on how sensitive you are in that particular area. With some people you are completely open, and with others, "selectively" open. Depending on the relationship, you may opt to share more things with certain people, and less with others. The size, or scope, of your open self depends entirely on your personality. It is common knowledge that some people are more open about themselves than others. People who do not share opinions or feelings are usually thought of as shy, although this may not be the case at all. They may simply be unwilling to share with certain people, and very willing with others.

The **blind self** represents the knowledge and information that others have about you, but you do not have, or know, about yourself. There are many habits that each of us have. We are aware of some, but unaware of others. There is the story of "Jane"who did not realize she had the nervous tendency of pulling out her eyelashes until she had none left.An unconscious gesture, she was sure it was everyone else's imagination. She would have sworn to the fact that she never did such a stupid thing. It only took looking in the mirror one day to make her realize that no one else had done it to her. Many nail biters fall into the same category. They are reminded by others that they have the habit, and may *know* that they do it, but they don't know *when* they do it, or *how often.*

The blind self might also include those things that you are unaware of psychologically because they happened at a much earlier time in your life. You may be an extremely insecure person - a person that feels unloved - yet unaware of the reasons why. Upon close analysis, you may tell yourself that you have a great relationship with your parents and friends, that you love them, and get nothing but love in return, so why those feelings of insecurity?

In the case of "Jack," he found out that a lifetime of feeling unloved was due to a grandfather who had treated him very badly as a child. A grandfather who told him he was worthless, stupid, silly, and would probably amount to nothing in life. What is interesting in this case is that Jack's grandfather died when Jack was four years old. He did not even remember the man, no less remember the verbal abuse he had put up with. It was only through years of therapy, and finally a confrontation with other members of his family, that Jack realized what had happened when he was so small. One man had taken a young, impressionable child, and made him feel that he was unlovable, and this feeling had lasted for thirty nine years, preventing and destroying most of his relationships.

The **hidden self** represents all the knowledge that you have about yourself, but that you do not share with others. Put simply, they are your secrets. They may include things that you are ashamed of, things that you dream or fantasize about, or those things that you feel are nobody else's business. Similar to the open self, you are selective concerning who you tell certain things to, and what you decide to tell them. A friend may be the perfect person to confide in regarding a failing exam, but you may not run to openly tell your parents.

The **unknown self** represents the part of you that resides in your subconscious. They are the things that you are unaware of, and others know nothing about. It is possible to go through life not understanding many things about yourself, but it is just as feasible that you learn these things through counseling, dreams, and psychological testing. Another way of understanding this rather vague part of who you are is examining and checking yourself with the help of people you care for and trust. This may be helpful for those people who feel uncomfortable about seeking any type of professional assistance- after all, counseling is not for everyone. The important thing to understand here is that you may be able to learn about those shadowy areas if you want to, but more interesting is the fact that due to this unknown area, you should *never say never.*

Increasing Self-Awareness and Self-Esteem

One of the many possible keys to your success is understanding who you are, and why you feel the way you do about yourself. If you feel secure, and believe that you can succeed in life, the chances are that much greater that you will succeed. If you consider yourself a failure, you may follow that path to the end of the line. The following represents a few tips to increase your self- awareness and self-esteem:

Build on your successes - When in doubt, think of all the things that you have done successfully in your life. Keep in mind that no one succeeds in everything all the time. Everyone meets with failure - it's how you react to that failure that determines whether you will allow yourself to try again. It's like the old story about falling off the horse...everyone knows that the best thing to do is to pick yourself up, brush yourself off, and get back on that horse. Failure is pretty much the same - just pick yourself up, swallow your fear, and try again. Don't allow yourself to become the kind of person who complains about all the things they could have done, should have done, and would have done. Remember the successes, think of the possibilities, and keep trying.

Look for positive people - Seek out the type of people who make you feel good about yourself. Hanging on to "friends" who remind you of your failures will not put you in the proper frame of mind for eventual success. Keep in mind that people who are down on themselves, and who expect to fail in life, tend to want to keep everyone else down with them. This does not mean that they are bad or spiteful people - it means that they are probably fearful of someone else's success reminding them of their own failures. Seek out those people who believe in, and think highly of you.

Believe in Yourself - Try to think of yourself in positive ways. Very few people think they're perfect, and they are probably right. There is no shame in the fact that we all have flaws. The shame is in not being able to see past those flaws to what is good, and decent, and worthwhile in all of us. As silly as it may sound, tell yourself once in a while that you're special; that you're as good as the next person, and deserve the best that life has to offer. It's just as easy to say "I can" as it is to say "I cant." Always concentrate on your potential, and not on your limitations.

Don't expect to be loved all the time - One of the most difficult things in life is to have to face the fact that no matter how nice you think you are, there will always be people who won't like you. This is particularly difficult in those situations where you try to please others. There is nothing wrong with your seeking love and approval; just remember that you won't always get it.

Be prepared and willing to self-disclose - The ability to understand yourself and share with others has many benefits. The most pertinent ones are:

Improvement of communication with others - There are certainly times in your life when keeping a secret will be to your advantage. There are, however, just as many times that expressing your thoughts, opinions, fears, or doubts may alleviate any number of misunderstandings. Speaking up has a tendency to "clear the air" and paves the way for more meaningful relationships. Remember: If you are willing to talk to others, they, in turn, will be willing to open up and talk to you.

A feeling of well-being - Don't ever minimize the importance of your mental health. Many people tend to view the word "health" as a physical manifestation only. It is not. Carrying around fear, anger and despair within you may be every bit as debilitating as a physical illness. Talk to people who you trust; talk to people who you care for - you'll feel much better about it.

The sense that you can cope with problems better - Regardless of how intelligent you may be, everyone needs to discuss certain aspects of their life with others. If nothing else, these discussions pave the way for looking at yourself through the eyes of others by actually giving you a new perspective. Groups such as Al-anon and Overeaters Anonymous thrive because people get the opportunity to openly discuss their problems with others, while learning that they are not alone in their struggle.

Chapter 3

Interpersonal Communication
"How Well Do We Get Along ?"

How do you perceive yourself? Do you see yourself as a happy, contented, well adjusted person,? Are you frustrated, and angry most of the time? Do you see the world as a kind place, or as a hostile, unfriendly place to live? The type of person you are, and how you ultimately feel about - or see - yourself, depends on many factors: how and where you were raised; who raised you; your formative (childhood) years, as well as many psychological and physical factors. We can safely say that the way you perceive yourself will greatly influence how you see others and relate interpersonally to them.

To learn more about ourselves and see why we relate to people the way we do, we must understand that "we" are made up of certain parts: **1. Our physical self** describes how we think, act, and react in terms of our physical well-being. An example here would be two people who come down with a bad case of the flu. One person lies in bed depressed, miserable, and complaining bitterly, whereas the other one - with exactly the same symptoms - makes light of the whole situation, and tries (in vain) to go about their business. Why would this happen? Perhaps the most simplistic answer is that one person has - by their very nature - a higher tolerance of pain and suffering. **2. Our intellectual self** describes how we feel about
capabilities - in other words, whether we think of ourselves as smart, and quick to pick up new things; or slow, and incapable of remembering and/or learning things. **3. Our emotional self** describes how we deal with our feelings and emotions. Some people are highly emotional, and deal with others in an erratic, almost childish fashion, due to their inability to look at the situation with their heads rather than their hearts. Whether a person is

emotional, or for that matter, lacking in emotion, goes back to their particular biological makeup as well as their childhood. Keep in mind that there are other "selves" that make you who you are: religious, moral, environmental, sexual, and monetary (why are some people so giving, whereas others are so stingy?).

Exercise - To understand a little more about yourself and how that self either remains constant, or changes, draw a bulls eye target map. Start with a small circle followed by another, and then another, increasing the perimeter until you have five or six circles. Now that your circles are complete, decide which of your various "selves" is the most crucial, or non-changing to you, and place that self in the center circle. In other words, if you placed your physical self in the center, that would mean that your whole life is wrapped around your physical well-being - how you feel; how you look; how often you get a chance to exercise; your diet, etc. The physical self for you would be, in essence, the core of your life, and would therefore greatly effect those around you. Place your other selves in the outer circles to determine what is important to you, (your core beliefs) and what is not.

The interesting point to be made with this exercise is that depending on the day, and depending on your particular mood, the circles may alter in terms of which self is the primary focus of your life. What is important to you in December may not necessarily be as important to you in July. What does all this mean? Put simply, it means that we are different people at different times, in different places. Those of us who accept these changes, and understand that they are a normal part of life, will ultimately fare better in terms of our interpersonal relationships.

Facilitating Relationships

A **facilitating relationship** is one in which the parties involved help each other. Each is as responsible as the other for the success or failure of the relationship. Some examples are mother and child; brother and sister; minister and parishioner; boyfriend and girlfriend. It may appear that these one-on-one relationships are easier than those where many people are involved, but nothing could be further from the truth. In a crowd, we can usually find at least one other person who shares our feelings, attitudes, and beliefs; at least one other person who will stick up for us and say that we are right. When dealing with a person one-on-one, conflicts are bound to arise. Most people like to be right; they usually believe that their way of thinking is the correct way, and at times, will fight to the finish until their beliefs are accepted. In a facilitating relationship, both parties involved would, by necessity, have to work out their problems or disagreements in order for the relationship to continue on an even keel.

In Chapter 2, there was a discussion of the attitudes and values that each of us have. We look once again at these particular aspects of who we are in terms of how we deal with others interpersonally.

Attitudes

Attitudes relate to a person's feelings, or position, with regard to another person or thing. Some attitudes are formed early in life and are dependent on such factors as the home environment, where the person lives, (the actual city, state, or country), and who they become friendly with. It may be said that an attitude is a function. Think of a math problem. You know that six plus six is twelve. The function in this problem is the <u>plus</u>. If you had been asked to figure out six <u>times</u> six, or six <u>minus</u> six, you realize that the answer would have been different. Relationships are like this too. If you speak to someone in a hostile tone, there's a better than even possibility that he/she will respond similarly. In other words, your attitude toward that person, or toward the situation, will effect their attitude toward you.

<u>Exercise</u> - To understand how your attitude effects your interpersonal relationships, divide the class in half (participants and observers), and imagine the following scenario: A sixteen year old girl has just shoplifted an expensive sweater from a neighborhood store. The manager caught her in the act, leaving no doubt as to her guilt. The girl is indignant, knowing full well that her parents are very good customers, and challenges the manager to call them. The question is how to handle both the girl, and the situation. Now imagine how the outcome will vary if you were to role-play the scenario in the following ways:
1. Manager is hostile, belligerent; Girl is unwilling to deal with the situation.
2. Manager is torn, uncertain what to do; Girl states that nobody will care about what she did.
3. Manager is hurt; Girl is ashamed.
4. Manager doesn't care -neither does the girl.

Imagine your own role-playing scenario. Depending on how a situation is handled, the end-result will ultimately vary from person to person.

Values

Values are those things that are important to you, passed on by members of your family, friends, and other people in your life that you respect.

Exercise - Working with at least three other people, choose four topics to discuss that you feel each of you knows something about. Try to discuss each subject area thoroughly, and determine how important each one is to your life. Rate each subject from 1-4, with 1 being the most important, and 4 being the least important to you. What are the chances that each person in the group will rate the subject areas the same? It is important to understand that there are no right or wrong answers here. The significance of the subject will vary from person to person depending on how they were raised, who raised them, where they live, and who they are friendly with.

Self-Concept and Self Disclosure

Self-Concept and Self-Disclosure were discussed in Chapter 2, but should also be rightfully included in a discussion of interpersonal communication. How you feel about yourself (self-esteem), and what you decide to reveal to others about you, will invariably result in both good and bad consequences in terms of your dealings with other people.

Exercise - Think of something that you've done that you feel ashamed of. Does anyone know about it? Have you shared the information with more than two people? How did those people react? Did they react the way you thought they would? Were you satisfied that you did the right thing by confiding in them? Would you share these things with others again, or keep them to yourself?
Choose five people in the class and determine how you would go about making contact with them. What would you be willing to self-disclose about yourself, and why? Would you tell each person the same thing? What "picture" would you like to create about yourself in each of their minds?

Biases

Biases are your preferences - what you like, and what you don't like; what you feel strongly about, and what is relatively unimportant to you. Some people like classical music; others don't. Some people like to exercise; others find it too time-consuming, and not worth the effort. Some biases are easily overcome in terms of interpersonal relationships: You may dislike Chinese food, but will give in to your friends who do like it by going to eat with them. Other biases are not as easily overcome because they mean more to you - in a sense, there is more at stake.

Consider the following questions in terms of your biases: Do you feel that there should be equality within a marriage? What are your views on mothers who go back to work immediately after having a child? What should be done about the homeless? Do you believe in the death penalty? Do you believe in reincarnation, or some form of life after death? Answering any, or all of these questions would ultimately lead to your disclosing a great deal of information about yourself. It might also lead to a good deal of disagreement between you and whoever else is involved in the discussion.

Despite our age, or level of intelligence, each of us tend to think that our point of view is the correct way of thinking. Sometimes it becomes impossible to "connect" with those people who disagree with us on certain matters, and this may ultimately lead to a breakdown in the communication process. Is there a simple remedy for this situation? Probably not. Is there anything that can be done at all? Yes. Tolerance is the answer- understanding and respecting others' viewpoints, and hoping that they understand and respect yours.

Exercise - Form a group of five to seven people, and discuss the following statement: "Animal experimentation is necessary for the ultimate welfare of humanity". After discussing thoroughly with the other members of the group, make a list and analyze those things that you agreed with, those things you disagreed with, and those things that you could possibly modify in terms of your biases.

Did you find that you were able to be more open-minded, and less judgmental? Did you find that you were provided with a few new insights? Did you find that nothing much changed at all in terms of how you felt? Did you listen critically to what the others had to say? Did you find that you had no opinion at all?

Projecting

In any interpersonal relationship, there are times when we **project** our feelings and thoughts onto others. We make the assumption that the other person feels the same way that we do; that they believe what we believe; that they will react the same way we will in a particular situation. Imagine your closest friend confiding in you that their four year relationship was about to end. You are fully aware of the circumstances, understand why the whole thing is happening, and tell your friend that "it's probably for the best." Instead of thanking you for your compassion and support, your friend - the person you thought you knew so well - gets upset (or angry) at your assumption that this is the way the relationship should have ended up. It's as if all the signals got crossed, and there's no connection. Projecting your feelings and thoughts on others reveals a great deal about your particular evaluating habits, and each of us should be aware of this potential problem when dealing with others. It's rare that one person feels *exactly* the same as another regardless of how close they are, or how well they know each other.

Exercise - Form a group of five people. One of the group members will be a reporter, another will be the person being questioned and observed, and the other three members of the group will be the witnesses. After being questioned about an important issue, (this can be decided upon by the group members beforehand) each person in the group should write down their reactions concerning what they had been told - what they believed they heard, what they thought the person meant by their statements. The idea here is that each person will probably have something different to say, some "twist" on what they thought they heard and perceived about the persons statements. In other words, we tend to project our own feelings, beliefs, and opinions, on others.

Validating Behavior

There are times in each of our lives that we look to others to **validate**, or affirm, our behavior. According to the dictionary, the actual word means "to legalize, confirm, or give approval to." A simple nod of the head, a smile, or a wink, may be all that is needed to give us a feeling of security and acceptance. In a sense, what we are looking for is to be told - either verbally or nonverbally - that we are right; that our way of thinking is correct; that we are not being rejected. An example of this would be John's taking an exam, feeling it was both difficult and unfair, and ultimately doing poorly. His asking other students in the class whether they felt the exam was hard is his way of validating his feelings and beliefs. Hopefully, John will get the positive reinforcement he needs by others agreeing with him.

Exercise - Write a short paragraph explaining your feelings about validating behavior. Are you the kind of person who needs others to tell you that you're right? Why is it that we need an element of commonality? In your opinion, does validating behavior help or hinder the communication process?

Fear of Rejection/Fear of Being Hurt

Regardless of how strong we think we are; regardless of our ability to build a wall of protection around ourselves, each of us has a fear of being rejected or hurt at some point in our lives. Some of us can only be hurt by people who we care about; others can just as easily be hurt by the comments or actions of strangers. The question here is how this fear projects itself in terms of our dealings with others. If each of our statements are modified so that we are not hurt, and so we don't hurt others, will this ultimately effect our relationships?, and if so, is this a good thing? We need to be aware of the fact that our actions/words are never isolated. Everything we do or say will trigger a response or action in someone else. It is also important to remember that regardless of how nice or kind we are, how "good" and helpful we try to be, there are times in our lives when we will be hurt, and inadvertently will hurt others.

Evaluations and Judgments

When we **evaluate** someone, or something, we are taking a positive step towards understanding what is going on. We are looking for specific reasons and possible answers to a situation. When we make a **judgment** however, we are taking a negative step by simply basing our opinions on previous knowledge, past experiences, and feelings. We are simply jumping to conclusions.

Exercise- Imagine the following scenario: Ken is sitting in class with twenty other students. The teacher tells everyone to open their books to page 48. Everyone does - except Ken. How do you react to this? Do you automatically judge him and make the assumption that Ken is being disrespectful, or obstinate? Do you say to yourself that he's a troublemaker who will do anything for attention- even if it's negative attention?, or do you evaluate the situation first by questioning*why* Ken did not open the book. When you evaluate a situation, you think it out clearly; when you judge a situation, you have a tendency to jump to conclusions.

Passive, Assertive, Aggressive Behavior

Have you ever been involved in a relationship where you felt that you had been "done in"; that you had been wronged, or slighted, or humiliated? If so, you probably reacted to the situation in one of three ways: passively, assertively, or aggressively.

When people behave **passively**, they do little, or nothing to work out, or change, the situation. They are either reluctant, or afraid, to state their opinions and feelings, and would just as soon let the whole incident slide. Unfortunately, this type of behavior may lead to future insults, as well as others taking advantage of the fact that this type of person "won't fight back." In some cases, it may appear that the person who reacts passively just does not care about the outcome - but feeling one way, and the reaction to that feeling - will vary from person to person.

When someone acts **assertively**, they describe their feelings, clearly explain their actions, discuss possible remedies, and take personal responsibility without attacking others. Put simply, it's a way of hopefully getting what you want, when you want it - *nicely*. It's telling someone that you're angry and hurt, without knocking some teeth out of their mouth.

When you act **aggressively**, you lash out blindly, without understanding or fear about the possible consequences. You don't think; you act.. You do not take responsibility for your actions, since your actions are ill-conceived.

Exercise 1 - With a group of about five people, analyze the following situation in terms of how it could be handled passively, assertively, and aggressively. Try to determine which behavior pattern would best accomplish achieving a "happy ending."

Nadine has been working at the hospital for fifteen years in her capacity as Executive secretary. All of her evaluations have been excellent, she is well respected, well liked, and considered to be a "high achiever." A position has just opened up in the head administrator's office which would elevate both Nadine's standing in the hospital, as well as her paycheck. She applies for the position, knowing full well that she can handle the pressure and the responsibility, but loses out to a young, less experienced woman who has been at the hospital for three years. What should Nadine do? What are her options?

Exercise 2 - Look at the following statements and determine which ones represent passive, assertive, or aggressive behavior:

1. I don't care where we go for dinner - you decide.
2. We must visit my aunt today.
3. I would prefer eating at the diner because I just had pizza.
4. I know you're busy, but I'd really appreciate speaking to you now rather than later.
5. You'll do your homework now - not tomorrow.
6. Maybe I'll call Peter today and apologize.
7. I would rather go to Puerto Rico on vacation rather than Aruba since we've been to Aruba three times already.

Summarizing the three contrasting behavior patterns, we find that assertive people have the greatest likelihood of achieving their goals. They are forceful without being abusive, confident without being haughty, and caring without allowing themselves to be treated like doormats.

Praise and Criticism

Everyone loves to be praised; few of us like to be criticized. When we work hard, and do something well, each of us needs an occasional pat on the back, or a look of respect from others. Many times a simple word or gesture is not given, however, and our self-respect and self-esteem may suffer. Why is it that some people find it easy to pass a compliment, whereas others would not dream of saying something nice to another person? One simplistic answer comes to light -jealousy. People who are secure within themselves, who feel confident about their talents, are generally able and willing to graciously extend accolades to others. Those of us who are insecure, or "down on ourselves," tend to be resentful towards other people's accomplishments thereby begrudging them a rightful word or gesture of praise. If you think about it, saying a few nice things to someone never hurts, but could ultimately help foster a friendship that otherwise would have been missed.

One way to improve upon your interpersonal communication skills is to ask for criticism. The problem is that you may ask for it, but not really want it. Imagine asking a close friend - someone you respect and care for - whether you tend to be obnoxious every time you speak to "Jeff." You're putting yourself in the position of hearing that you *do* tend to be abrasive, short, and snotty with him. Do you really want to hear it? You should. If you know the person you're speaking with is not out to hurt you, but rather to help you...take advantage of the moment, and learn something about yourself. Swallow your pride, admit that perhaps you handled a situation badly, and move on from there.

Responses that create problems

Some of us communicate very effectively. We think before we speak, listen critically to others, evaluate situations before jumping to conclusions, pass compliments when they are deserved, and support our family and friends in word and deed. So what's the problem? *We all make mistakes.* Sometimes they are intentional, most of the time we are unaware of the fact that we are doing or saying something wrong.

Interrupting responses occur when we finish a statement for another person. We automatically assume that we are smart enough to know what's going to be said...so we say it. Sometimes we're right about what the person was going to say, and sometimes we're wrong - but in either case, it should not have happened. Interrupting someone shows a lack of sensitivity, and in some cases displays a superior attitude - as if to say: "Don't bother to finish, because I already know what you have to say."

Irrelevant responses are those statements that have absolutely nothing to do with the conversation. You ask your brother if he knows what you're having for dinner, and he responds by saying how his football team is first in the county. An irrelevant response is one where the sender of the message is ignored completely. Once again, as in the case of the interrupting response, a person may wonder whether what they are asking/saying has any importance whatsoever.

Incongruous responses usually deal with conflicting messages. Imagine telling someone that you were basically pleased with the grade of C that you received in Math, and their responding sarcastically by saying, "Sure, a C is definitely something to be satisfied with." Incongruous responses may be sarcastic, stemming from a misunderstanding of the meaning of the message, and may lead to a breakdown in communication.

Tangential responses are those statements that don't quite seem to address or deal specifically with the issue at hand. It's as if you're speaking about the same topic, but from another angle. I tell you that in my opinion Michael Jackson has probably gone too far in his quest to look like someone/something else. You respond by saying that your Uncle Simon has had a lot of plastic surgery lately. Are we both talking about changing an image? Yes. Are we both talking about the same person? No.

Getting along with, and dealing with other people is not always the easiest thing to do. Being aware of potential communication problems can therefore pave the way for a greater measure of success.

Chapter 4

Listening
"Listen Up, Please"

Imagine this: Your friend has just told you what time they would like to meet for dinner. You smile, walk away, and realize within five minutes that you don't know when you're supposed to meet. Is there something wrong with you? Doubtful. Chances are, you are one of the countless millions of people who thought you were listening, but weren't. You assumed that because you heard what your friend said (hearing), that you understood, and were paying attention to what was being said (listening). In this chapter, we will investigate the process of listening, and the strategies for improving our listening skills.

Many of us take listening for granted. Because it is something that we have done naturally all our lives, we don't bother to give it much thought. Unlike learning to play a sport like soccer or golf, where there are definite rules, procedures, and goals, we don't feel that listening requires any work at all. According to Dr. Ralph Nichols, the "father of listening," people function at only 25% of their actual listening capacity. Assuming that this is true for most people, we are not actually good listeners at all. With this fact in mind, it would make sense to believe that working toward improving this skill is crucial. A study, conducted in 1975 by Elyse Wener, showed the following:

* 70% of our waking time is spent communicating; of that 70%:
* 9% is spent on writing
* 12% is spent on reading
* 25% is spent on speaking
* 54% is spent on listening

Think of all the people in your life, and try to assess how

carefully you listen to each of them. Do you listen more to your mother, or to your father; or don't you listen to either of them? Do you listen more critically to your boss, or to your teachers? To your friends, or to your doctor? Naturally, each of us will have different answers depending on who, or what we place the most importance on. Since we spend so much of our communication time listening to others, it would make sense to improve our skills in that area. Let's examine the reasons why we may not be as good at listening as we think we are, and discuss the ways in which we can achieve a greater level of listening proficiency:

1. **Boredom**	6. **Emotions**
2. **Noise**	7. **Tune-Out**
3. **Difficult Material**	8. **Questioning**
4. **Notetaking**	9. **Criticism**
5. **Posture and Movement**	10. **Daydreaming**

1. Boredom - Everyone gets bored once in a while. There are times when getting bored won't effect our lives at all, and other times when it will. Getting bored on the job, and slacking off, might be the beginning of the end for you in that particular profession; Getting bored in your classes may ultimately lead to your inability to receive a decent grade. The important point here is for you to understand that you may ultimately get bored at the most inconvenient times, so you should be prepared to do something about it:

<u>Ineffective Habits</u> -You put your head on the desk sitting motionless, in a catatonic state, because you're tired, not interested in the material, or find that it's totally meaningless.

<u>Listening Goals</u> - Find an area of interest related to yourself. If you can make something about the subject important to you, you'll listen more critically, and remember things more readily. Remember to ask yourself this question: What could possibly be in this for me?

2. Noise - Most people associate the word "noise" with something that is very loud and annoying. In terms of our communication skills, the word takes on a broader meaning. For our purposes, noise is anything that interferes with, or distorts, a message. **Physical noise** is the distortion of sound - your inability to hear a friend in a crowded, noisy room, or static on your radio. **Semantic noise** refers to the distortions that occur due to the lack of comprehension of other people's words. **Psychological noise** refers to the distortions created by our own prejudices. **Biological noise** refers to the "noise of the body" - a headache, stomach ache, back ache, or hangover.

Ineffective Habits - You get easily distracted by outside noises such as people passing by the door and talking; the rustling of the leaves on a cool, spring day; your stomach telling you that you are in need of food.

Listening Goals - Acknowledge that you are being distracted by something; whether it is internal noise (your hunger pangs) or external noise (others talking, loud sounds,) remind yourself that those distractions can be easily overcome by "thinking through them." - forgetting them for the moment, and concentrating on the task at hand.

3. Difficult Material - At times, even the most intelligent people find themselves steering clear of difficult material. If at all possible, why not find an easy way of learning or remembering something? It's only natural to take shortcuts. The only problem is that it's not always possible to do so.

Ineffective Habits - You prefer listening to light material...things that are fun, recreational, and pleasant. You're fairly certain that anything taxing to your brain will not hold your attention, and you don't want to expend any unnecessary energy.

Listening Goals - Exercise your mind by exposing yourself to heavier, more difficult material. Force yourself to focus in more clearly to information that's hard to understand. Have a positive outlook, and tell yourself that you can understand and appreciate things that put a little pressure on your brain.

4. Notetaking - Considering all the potential problems that may arise when trying to take notes, it is apparent that altering, or modifying, your notetaking system may be helpful.

Ineffective Habits - You attempt - unsuccessfully - to write down every word that your teacher says; your hand cramps easily, so you don't take any notes at all; you can't spell very well, and your grammar is terrible...so why bother; you can't listen and write at the same time; you write too slowly, and your handwriting is terrible; you forgot to bring in any writing material; your teacher speaks too rapidly, and you can't write that quickly.

Listening Goals - First and foremost, learn how to paraphrase material. Listen carefully to what is being said, and then put it in your own words. Since it is virtually impossible to get down every word spoken (unless you take shorthand), the next best thing is to grasp the concept, and write it down in your own fashion - in a way

that will make it easier for you to study at a later date. For those of
you who are particularly poor at notetaking, a tape recorder might
do the trick. This will allow you the freedom of paying closer
attention in class, without getting bogged down by writers' cramp.
If you're the type of person who likes the sound of your own voice,
you may want to try reading some chapters of a book into a tape
recorder, and then listening to yourself at a time that is more
convenient for you. Last, but not least, you may want to take the
notes that you have, and put them in outline form...keeping it short,
and sweet in order to study later.

Notetaking takes time and a great deal of energy, but will
definitely improve in time by utilizing one or more of the systems
mentioned. Keep in mind that some of the ideas may work for you,
and others won't. Don't make any judgments based on what other
people say. Each individual works and learns in their own unique
fashion. Find what suits you best, and then work on the skill
keeping in mind that " practice makes perfect" - the more you do
something, the better you get at it.

5. Posture and Movement -   The way you sit in a
classroom, at a meeting, or in an office, may have a great effect on
your listening effectiveness. If you are one of the countless
numbers of people who exhibit ineffective posture and movement
habits, you are probably not expending the energy necessary to
listen effectively.

Ineffective Habits - You have the habit of placing yourself in
the back of a room so that you can lean against the wall; you lean
forward with your head in your hands; you tap your fingers
repeatedly on the desk; you keep one leg crossed over the other;
any other repetitive gesture such as nail biting, or twirling your hair.

Listening Goals - You need to work on your body state by
following three easy steps: 1.Plant both feet firmly on the ground.
2. Make sure that there is at least one inch of space between your
lower back and your seat. 3. Place your hands on opposite sides of
the desk with one hand higher than the other. Although it may
sound a little ridiculous, the more comfortable you are in your seat,
the less likely you are to be able to listen effectively. Anyone
speaking to you - a friend, parent, or teacher - gets feedback based
on your body positions, head motions, eye contact, and facial
expressions. Be aware of this fact, and work on your body state.

6. Emotions - Nobody likes to be interrupted when they are
speaking - especially if they think they're talking about something
interesting; a few of us (maybe a lot of us) get upset, or even

antagonized, by people who disagree with what we have to say. Depending on our individual personalities, we react differently to people who irritate us, and this will ultimately effect whether we listen to them or not. Test your own "irritation level" by answering the following questions:

1. Y__ N__ Do you find that you interrupt people often?
2. Y__ N__ Do you stop listening to someone when you don't like what's being said?
3. Y__ N__ Do you get into arguments easily?
4. Y__ N__ Do you find that there are certain words that "tick you off?"
5. Y__ N__ Do you get angry when you feel people are not listening to you?
6. Y__ N__ Do you get upset when you can't seem to get your message across to others?
7. Y__ N__ Do you stop listening to others when you are upset about things going on in your life?

If you answered "yes" to most of these questions, then you may need to analyze your own emotional state before dealing with others, or at the very least, be aware of the fact that you're not able to "give your all" due to your own problems or prejudices.

Ineffective Habits - The questions above clearly delineate the habits that may lead to your listening ineffectiveness- arguing too often with people; interrupting others; turning off to people because you don't like what they have to say; letting your own personal problems effect what's going on with others.

Listening Goals - We need to learn the skill of "holding"- hold your thoughts; hold your judgments; hold your answers; and hold your anger. Wait to receive the entire message before getting upset; try not to interrupt (you wouldn't want it done to you); and try to remain open-minded about what's being said. Keep in mind that in any type of communication endeavor where there are two or more people involved, there are bound to be disagreements. Each of us comes into a relationship with our own set of emotional " baggage;" each of us get upset about some things, and let other things slide; each of us has our own level of tolerance. If we can extend the same level of courtesy and understanding to others that we would expect and like for ourselves, listening will become a pleasant experience.

7. Tune-Out - There are many reasons why people tune out on a fairly regular basis. This does not necessarily mean that they are rude, or lacking in intelligence, but rather a matter of their having something else more important to think about.

<u>Ineffective Habits -</u>   You find yourself tuning out to what is being said in class, and have a great deal of difficulty tuning back in because you have more pressing concerns on you mind.

<u>Listening Goals -</u>   Try to focus on visual cues. In order to do this, you must maintain eye contact with the speaker; decide the relative importance of the message being sent, and focus; try to associate what's being said with someone you know, somewhere you've been, or something you want to know more about; be aware of your personal space in the classroom by trying to position yourself away from the walls, windows, and door. If possible, try to position yourself front and center; when you miss some information by "blanking out", don't consider it a total loss - re-focus, and then try to fill in the missing pieces. Always determine the worth of anything you are listening to by connecting the ideas with how they relate to you personally. In other words, try to find some relevance and importance in everything that you listen to.

8. Questioning - The more you ask, the more you learn. It's that simple. If you prepare yourself to ask questions, you will be in a better position to listen more critically for the answers.

<u>Ineffective Habits</u> - There are four main reasons why people do not ask questions; 1. They are just too lazy to bother because they really don't care enough about what's being said. 2. They don't really know *what* to ask. 3. They are embarrassed, or shy, about asking questions because they don't want to draw any unnecessary attention to themselves. 4. They feel that the questions they ask will make them look foolish.

<u>Listening Goals -</u>   In order to prepare yourself to ask questions, it would help to break down the message that is being sent into three distinct categories: the theme (the whole picture); the ideas within the theme; the facts supporting those ideas. Once you understand that there are specific things you should be listening for, you will be able to focus in more clearly on the actual message, thereby allowing you the possibility of formulating questions. Some typical questions that may be asked are: 1. Can you give me another example? 2. Would you please go over that definition one more time? 3. Can you possibly put that idea another way? (paraphrase it) 4. Am I right when I say that_____? 5. Can I assume that if ____ happens, then _____will probably happen also? 6. Could another example of this theme be_____?.

Probably the best reason to ask questions is that it forces you to listen more critically to what's going on in order to formulate what to ask, but another reason is that it's usually very helpful to others. They are undoubtedly just as uncomfortable as you are about asking questions, and you would be doing the job for them!

9. Criticism - In order to understand the value, or potential harm, of criticism, (judging) we must first identify two definitions: 1. Constructive criticism - This type of criticism is positive, and its aim is to be helpful. It is never mean-spirited, and is usually done out of love, friendship, kindness, and understanding 2. Destructive criticism - pretty much the opposite of constructive criticism in every way; it is meant to hurt; it is done out of anger, frustration, fear, or prejudice; it is spiteful; it shows a lack of compassion and understanding. In terms of our listening effectiveness, destructive criticism shows that we are turning off more to the person speaking, rather than to what they are speaking about.

Ineffective Habits - For the most part, destructive criticism gets us no place. It is the rare person who will smile, shake your hand, and thank you for insulting or hurting them. Some of us are lucky enough to have the knack of being able to say something negative in a way that does not hurt people, but some of us don't have that particular ability. Look at the following statements, and decide whether you would answer True or False:

1. T___ F___ I judge a person by the way he/she dresses.
2. T___ F___ I usually stop listening to people when they start talking about things that I've never heard about before.
3. T___ F___ I find myself turning off to people who speak with an accent because they are too difficult to understand.
4. T___ F___ When things are left open to interpretation, I get confused and turn off to the person.
5. T___ F___ Sometimes I understand all the words that are said, but somehow miss the content.
6. T___ F___ I will not listen to someone if they are boring.
7. T___ F___ If I think you're not too bright, I won't bother to listen to you.
8. T___ F___ I feel superior to certain people.

If you answered True to most of the eight statements, then you are the type of person who tends to be overly critical of others, impatient, and possibly prejudiced. You need to analyze yourself in terms of how you would feel if others reacted to you this way.

<u>Listening Goals</u>-Criticism is a natural part of life. It would be a wonderful world if everyone liked and respected one another, but unfortunately, it does not seem to work out that way. The important thing is to know how, and when, to criticize by understanding your own listening prejudices. In all of our interpersonal communication situations, we have three listening "selves."

1. *The identifying listening self* - The person sitting next to you in class fails an exam; you can easily identify with and understand how they are feeling because you've been there.

2. *The sympathetic listening self* - You identify with and understand another persons problem, and feel badly about it.

3. *The empathic listening self* - You identify with, understand, and feel badly enough for the other person so that you are able to "put yourself in their shoes." Because of your emotional response to their problem, you are able to offer constructive criticism.

Try to understand that opening yourself up, and understanding what's going on with the other person will lead to your becoming a non-evaluative listener - someone who thinks first before judging and responding to others; someone who listens for the content of the message, rather than to the person who is sending it.

10. Daydreaming - If asked whether daydreaming was a negative behavior pattern, most people would say "yes." If caught doing it by a friend, teacher, or employer, you would probably apologize. After all, it does seem rude to be thinking of something else when someone is speaking to you. The truth is, daydreaming is perfectly normal. We are able to listen to people four times faster than they speak; which means that we have spare time for our thoughts to wander. The problem with daydreaming is that we wander too far for too long.

<u>Ineffective Habits</u> - You have a tendency to "space out" at the most inopportune moments. Lying on the beach and daydreaming usually does not have any dire consequences, (aside from losing touch with the time, and burning to a crisp) but daydreaming while at work, or in the classroom, can be embarrassing, and create problems that are a little more far-reaching.

<u>Listening Goals</u> - Even though daydreaming is a perfectly normal phenomenon, there are times when doing so can lead to problems. When you know that the timing is wrong for letting yourself drift off, try doing the following: 1.Realize that you *are* daydreaming. Tell yourself that your thoughts - regardless of how pleasant they are - can be held off for a better moment. 2. Attempt to come back to the here and now, and summarize what's been said.

Don't worry about the fact that you may have missed some of the material; missing some of it is still better than missing all of it. 3. Tell yourself that what you're listening to is important in some way. 4. Keep yourself involved in what's going on by guessing what might be coming next.

Make yourself an active, rather than a passive, part of the listening process. The more you're willing to give in terms of time and effort, the more you'll get in return.

Five Steps of the Listening Process

We have discussed the ten possible reasons why we might not be as effective at listening as we should be, and the ways to improve those skills. It would also help to understand the process of listening itself - a process that may seem to come naturally, without giving it a thought, our whole lives.

1. Reception (or Receiving)- The process of hearing. In order to listen, (pay attention) we must be able to hear. (sounds-auditory stimuli) For those people who are hearing impaired, this process is altered by the fact that they do not pick up auditory stimuli, but rather "see" the sounds that are being made through sign language. Listening begins with the receiving of the messages that are sent by the speaker .

2. Perception (or Understanding) - In this step, we try to make sense out of what is being said to us...in other words, we try to learn what the speaker means. This process of learning encompasses both the intellectual and emotional level of the message. We must " read between the lines" to determine not only the words, but the emotion behind those words. (Is the speaker angry, sad, hostile, or overcome with joy).

3. Remembering - It's one thing to receive and understand a message being sent to us, but another thing entirely to remember and retain what we've heard. This problem can easily be alleviated in a classroom situation by taking good notes, or by taping the material. In our everyday lives, however, we cannot rely on any aids to help us. We speak to people; they speak to us; and we try to remember all that's been said to us. Certainly there are many times in our lives when we hear what people are saying (sounds), but are not paying the slightest bit of attention to them (listening). This is usually done unconsciously, (we are preoccupied with other pressing thoughts) or out of choice (we don't like or respect the person speaking to us, so we just tune them out). It is interesting that we don't necessarily remember the things that are said to us, but what we *think* has been said to us. In other words, three people may listen to someone tell a story, yet each will relay the same tale in a different way depending on how they felt, or reacted to it.

There are many tricks to learning how to remember. One way is by constant repetition - such as when you memorize the words to a song, or the lines in a play. Another way to learn is mnemonically. **Mnemonics** is a way of remembering things by utilizing letters or words to make learning easier. One example of learning to remember mnemonically is thinking of the word "HOMES". Once you have that relatively easy word in your head, it becomes easier to remember what the letters stand for in terms of Geography: H - Huron; O - Ontario; M -Michigan; E - Erie; S - Superior. Learning the names of the five great lakes couldn't be simpler.

4. Evaluating - When you evaluate, you make a judgment about a message. If someone says that they're absolutely crazy about you, you have to determine (judge) whether they're setting you up to ask a favor; are being sarcastic; or simply like you a whole lot. Your feelings, and judgments, will be based in part on the relationship that you have with the person involved.

5. Responding - Our response to the message sent. It may be verbal, or nonverbal; it may be positive, or negative; it may be supportive, or non-supportive. Keep in mind that there is no such thing as *not* responding. You may listen to someone speak, and stand there like a statue (not speaking or moving) - but that in itself, is a response.

We listen to the people around us for many reasons: for knowledge, for enjoyment, for social acceptance, and in some cases, for power and status. The good listener should therefore be aware of the fact that this is probably the most important activity in terms of their interpersonal communication skills.

Chapter 5

Small Group Communication
"Am I A Team Player?"

A small group consists of three to twelve people who come together for the purpose of accomplishing a particular goal.Unlike other interpersonal situations, the group must function as a cohesive unit. There must be total involvement and interaction between each member of the group in order to achieve a measure of success. Each person should get the opportunity to verbally address the issue(s), and present their ideas and feelings.

A group functions best when they identify and define the problem, establish criteria for evaluating possible solutions, analyze the various arguments, and reach either a majority or unanimous decision. As in many interpersonal dealings, agreeing with people is not necessarily an easy task. Imagine the difficulty getting just one person to agree with you on certain issues - now multiply that number a few times. Learning about the various types of small group situations, and how decision-making can be accomplished efficiently and painlessly is the goal of this chapter.

Small Group Meeting Formats

Brainstorming Discussions - The group comes together without any prepared plan of action. Each person gets the opportunity to speak about a number of issues; about things that may be bothering them; things that they want to change; things that they want to keep the same. It's a " smorgasbord" of ideas that tends to be open-ended, and lacking in specificity. It should be understood that brainstorming discussions might ultimately lead to the groups honing in on a particular issue - but not necessarily.

Round Table Discussions - People come together for a specific purpose, with a specific goal in mind. The group interaction is informal, and is used by many large corporations to bring people together in a more relaxed comfortable, less tense, atmosphere.

Buzz Sessions - Usually used in a classroom-type setting where a large group is broken down into smaller groups for discussion of a particular topic.

Quality Circles - These are meetings that are set up between employees of a company /corporation /school to examine work-related problems. Once a viable solution is reached between the members of the group, the information is passed along to "upper management" for their consideration and approval.

Support Groups - This type of group is set up to help people who have a particular problem in common. As an example, new inexperienced parents can join a support group where they get the opportunity to air their problems and differences, as well as listening to others who may have similar concerns.The support group works as an invaluable tool for many of us who feel that we don't know all of the answers, or feel that we are not wise enough to handle things correctly. Listening and sharing with others usually makes us realize that *we are not alone.*

Study Groups - These groups are arranged so that students taking the same course can work together in order to increase their understanding of the subject area.

The Panel -This is a group of people who are each "experts" in their field. Similar to the round table type of discussion, the interaction is informal, discussions will be varied, and there are audience members involved who may ask questions and interject thoughts.

The Symposium -The most formal of all groups, there are a series of prepared speeches, each dealing with different aspects of a single issue, presented in front of an audience who may ask questions and make comments. There is a leader involved who introduces each of the speakers, and moderates the questions posed by audience members.

Goals of the Group

1. The problem, or issue, should be defined and analyzed.
2. Criteria should be established for the evaluation of solutions.
3. A number of solutions should be identified.
4. Those possible solutions should be evaluated.
5. The best solution should be selected.

Context of Small Groups

If you are waiting for a class to begin with a number of other people; if you're standing on line at the bank, or waiting for a bus, the people who are with you do *not* constitute a group. It must be understood that a group consists of those people who: 1. have an awareness of each others presence, 2. have some form of reciprocal influence on each other, and 3. have a common goal in mind.

The Individual Within the Context of the Group

1. Each person must decide to take an active part in, and be committed to, the ultimate success of the group.
2. Each person must be willing to assume leadership responsibilities.
3. Each person must assume that they will have a particular responsibility (function) within the group.
4. Each person must seek and give information: asking for facts, seeking clarification.
5. Each person must be willing to initiate activity: coming up with new and creative ideas, or discussing different perspectives of the issue.
6. Each person must show a degree of sensitivity to the norms and standards set up by the group, and to the individuals who abide by those rules.

Positive Behavior within the Group

The group is a working, cooperative unit. Each member should be oriented towards the group effort rather than the individual, and should deal with issues rather than personalities. The type of behavior that builds and strengthens this unit are:

Climate - making sure that the "aura" or feeling surrounding each member of the group is a comfortable one. Attempting to keep tensions from mounting by encouraging positive feedback, and reinforcing the good things within the group.

Gatekeeping - Exhibiting and maintaining open lines of communication between people through encouragement.

Harmonizing - The willingness of each group member to "keep the peace" by explaining, clarifying, and understanding the differences amongst themselves.

Compromising - Working as a team to resolve any conflict within the group through a willingness to "give in" (just a little) to each other.

Evaluating - Critically discussing and analyzing the decisions made by the group.

Dysfunctional Behavior within the Group

Sometimes, a member (or members) of a group may not play by the rules. This may be purposeful, or unintentional, but in either case, it serves to undermine the structure, purpose, and ultimate goal of the group.

Blocking - Providing negative feedback and opposing views which may hinder the group process and eventual outcome.

Self-recognition - The tendency of one or more group members to focus in on their particular concerns, problems, and feelings, rather than dealing with the overall needs of the group.

Competing - Working as an adversary (attacker) towards the group, and playing the game of "one upmanship."

Sympathy-seeker - Expressing one's insecurity within the context of the group by trying to get sympathy from others.

Horsing around - Not taking the group members or their goals seriously; making a joke of the situation.

Withdrawal - Showing a lack of interest and concern by retreating in silence from the rest of the group.

Function of Group Leaders

1. Helps each member function as a unit. Attempts to bring the group closer to their desired goals.
2. Initiates (starts) the discussion.
3. Helps to keep the group on the topic.
4. Facilitates communication between each member.

5. Shows that he/she values the beliefs and opinions of others.
6. Listens critically to each person.
7. Gives credit to others.
8. Shows a willingness to admit mistakes.
9. Has a sense of humor.

Styles of Leadership

Laissez-faire - This type of leader allows the group to move at their own pace. They can develop their own ideas and arrive at their own solutions without much interference.

Authoritarian - A leader who exercises complete control over the group. They determine what the problem is; how the group will proceed; what criteria will be used; what function or task each person will have within the group; makes decisions without the consent of the other members.

Democratic - Similar to the Laissez-faire type of leadership in terms of allowing the group to progress on its own, but the leader provides definite direction.

Exercises - The following situations call for a small group discussion to resolve the issues. Utilizing the information given in this chapter, form a group and see what conclusions you arrive at.

Situation 1 - You are a car salesman who prides yourself on knowing how to make a lot of money by being smart and merciless. Your neighbor comes into the showroom where you work and shows an interest in buying a car that looks great - you know, however, that the car is a good looking piece of junk...What do you do?

Situation 2 - You've been married for ten years to a great guy. You have two beautiful children who are both doing well in school and have lots of friends. The problem is that your husband is an alcoholic. Problems are beginning to creep up in his professional and personal life...What do you do?

Situation 3 - You work part-time in a men's clothing store. Someone you know from school comes into the store and starts looking around. He doesn't notice you, but you recognize him. Through a side mirror, you see him taking an expensive sweater and putting it under his jacket. He walks out...What do you do?

Situation 4 - Your seventeen year old daughter has just excitedly informed you that she has an opportunity to tour with a well respected band as their pianist. She explained that she would be gone for seven months with a possible option of continuing for another three months. You always assumed that her years of study would lead to her becoming a music teacher - and now this...What do you do? Do you feel she owes you anything for your time, effort, and financial support over the years? Is she too young to be considering this type of job?

Situation 5 - You just got a job at a fast-food restaurant, and realize to your surprise that a friend from school is your supervisor. You are happy about the situation because you like this person, and figure that your life will be much easier with her in charge. Within a month of your slacking off (just a little), your supervisor tells the manager that you should be fired...What do you do? Is this situation totally unreal? Do you know anyone who has had something similar happen to them?

Situation 6 - One of your closest friends has just bought you a very expensive, modern piece of glass for the unit in your family room. Although you appreciate the gesture, you really don't like the piece at all because you're basically an antique collector...What do you do? What do you say? Do you return the gift and say nothing? Do you keep it and just hide it in a closet? Do you tell your friend what you really think?

Situation 7 - There is a petition going around your neighborhood which - if signed by enough people - will eliminate the possibility of a new housing development for retarded people in your area. You are not opposed to the idea at all, but realize that most of your neighbors (some close friends included) don't want "those type of people near their kids, or on their streets."...What do you do? Do you go against your own personal beliefs to keep your friends and neighbors happy? Do you refuse to sign, and take your chances on how you will be treated?

Situation 8 - A family member who you have a wonderful relationship with is in the hospital. Everyone but the patient knows that he is dying of cancer. You walk into the room; he looks distressed; he asks you what's really happening -he trusts you, he knows you'll tell him the truth...What do you do? What do you say?

Chapter 6

The Verbal Message - Language
"What Did You Mean By That?"

Does this sound familiar to you? "I was having a conversation with a friend of mine, and I realized after I spoke that I should have said..." or, "If I had *only* said..." or, "If I ever got the chance again, I *would* say..." The problem is that too often, we don't get the chance to say it another way. There are times when it's just too late to take back what's already been said. The lesson to be learned here is that we should think before we speak, and when we do, make sure that our thoughts are clear, so that the verbal message is not misunderstood or misinterpreted.

Language is a means of communicating with one another. We communicate our ideas and our feelings through the use of sounds and symbols. A potential problem with language is that there are times when meanings get confused, and words are used incorrectly or inappropriately. Within families, or between friends, this does not happen as often, since there is an element of intuitive understanding- the people know each other so well that there is an overall comprehension. When dealing with strangers, or your employer, however, the words you speak should clearly convey your meaning.

Exercise - Design and develop a poster using language that best suits the understanding of your particular viewpoint. Choose one of the following subjects:

My Country
Poverty
Famine
The Homeless
Tanning Salons

When we speak, we do so in **message units**. Basically this means that we have a pattern to whatever it is that we say. It is rare that we speak using isolated words. The only time this happens is when we say "yes" or "no", and even then, we usually expound on the words by explaining *why* we said yes, or no.

Within the context of the spoken message unit, many people use **crutch phrases, or fillers.** How uh, many times, um, do you, ah, use these, uh, non-words? There are a number of reasons that people use crutch phrases: They use them to fill in the empty spaces between thoughts; They use them to allow time to consider what should be said next; They use them because they don't have a clue as to what they should say next (lack of preparation); They use them because they are nervous, and blank out. Whatever the reason, using these fillers is normal, and will happen to the best of us. Probably the easiest way to avoid the over-usage of the crutch phrase is to practice what you are going to say a number of times before actually presenting the material.

Exercise 1 - Imagine that you are auditioning for a role on your favorite television program. The casting director has asked you to present a one minute profile of yourself...explaining who you are, what your likes and dislikes are, and why you think you should be given the opportunity to be on T.V. Do not write your answer; be prepared to speak in an extemporaneous fashion using language that is clear, precise, and informative. Try not to use fillers; try not to repeat yourself.

Exercise 2 - Design a flyer for an opening event, using language that is colorful, exciting, and informative. Select an event of your own, or use the following ideas as examples:

1. A Broadway musical
2. The grand opening of a major department store
3. The opening of a new business
4. The opening of a new Disney-like theme park

The Nature of Language

Language allows each of us the freedom to explain things that have happened in the past, that are going on in the present, or to hypothesize about the future. It allows us to label, evaluate, define, and distort. Language can soothe, and it can hurt; it can be helpful, and it can be destructive. **Language can be emotional** - getting through to people through their hearts, rather than their heads;

Language may be factual - it can be verified; dealing with statistics, quotations, and other proven data. **Language may be opinionated-** statements or words that are based on feelings, gut reactions, and hypothetical guesswork. **Language may be heavy with propaganda** - goading us to buy or do things with enough misleading information to keep us guessing just how much is true. When speaking or listening, you should be aware of how language is being used so that the decisions you make, and the actions you take, are well chosen.

<u>Exercise</u> - With the understanding that the nature of language will vary depending on the necessity of the moment, create your own "sales pitch." Decide which tactic you will utilize to best sell your product/idea.

Denotative vs. Connotative Meanings

The **denotative** meaning of a word is the meaning that is shared by people who speak a specific language. As an example, if you were to look up the word "bad" in the Random House Dictionary of the English Language, you would find that it means, "not good in any manner or degree; of poor quality; morally reprehensible; inadequate, or below standard; defective in both quality and worth." In other words, the denotative meaning is the one we find in the dictionary - the one that we set a basic standard of understanding with- it is the objective meaning of the word The difficulty lies in the fact that we do not always speak denotatively. Depending on the era, the decade, the fad of the moment, we speak connotatively.

The **connotative** meaning of a word is the meaning that we give it subjectively or emotionally- in other words, it's the meaning that we feel like giving it. By the early 1980s, the word "bad" had taken on a new connotative meaning. If someone said you were bad, it could have meant that you had done something wrong, or that you were a low-life degenerate- but it also could have meant that you were something special (a definite cut above the rest), or that you had done something totally incredible, or unbelievable. In the 1960s, telling someone that they were "way out", meant pretty much the same thing as being told you were "bad" in the 1980s.

<u>Exercise</u> - It is said that " meanings are in people." With this in mind, look at the following words and determine what you consider

to be their connotative meanings. On a piece of paper write down as many meanings as you can think of.

1. Cool   4. Trip
2. Unreal   5. Square
3. Gay   6. Fast

Facts vs. Inferences

On the last page, we differentiated between fact and opinion - a fact being proven data, as compared to an opinion which dealt more with educated guesswork and emotions. An **inference** is similar to an opinion in that it is not necessarily based on factual material, but rather on those things that we feel - in our opinion - to be true, based on previous knowledge and observations.

As an example, let's imagine that your fourteen year old neighbor has a tendency to play loud rock music every night between eight and ten in the evening. It's a normal Wednesday night, and the music starts blaring at 8:00 P.M. The average person will automatically assume that it's the teenager whose stereo is blasting -he/she will make that *inference* . But is it a fact? Might it be that the music is coming from another apartment? from a visiting friend or relative? The point is that you may be right in assuming (inferring) where the music is coming from, but until all the facts are in, you can't be certain. If you are a critical listener, you will be able to differentiate between a statement of fact, and one of inference.

<u>Exercise</u> - Look at the following sentences, and determine whether each is a statement of fact or inference.

1. Joey is fat because he eats too much.
2. One of Columbus' ships was named the Santa Maria.
3. The Titanic sunk on its maiden voyage.
4. People who smoke heavily will die of lung cancer.
5. Yale University is in the state of Connecticut.
6. A college degree will ensure a good job after graduation.
7. People with I.Q.s above 150 will be successful in life.
8. Fifty plus fifty minus twenty equals eighty.
9. Reading one book per week will increase your SAT scores.
10. The Civil War ended in 1865.
11. A CD player utilizes a laser.

12. The American Revolution is discussed in all history books.
13. Skim milk has less fat than whole milk.
14. Albany is the capital of New York State.
15. The all-time snowfall record for New York City was in 1947 - until the new record of 27 inches on Jan.8, 1996.
16. He wears glasses; he must be intelligent.
17. That old man is stumbling around; he must be drunk.
18. She's well built, blond, and dresses provocatively; she must be just another bimbo.
19. There is no oxygen on Venus, so there is no possibility of life on that planet.
20. The earth travels around the sun.

Language Clarity

There are times when it becomes necessary for us to explain things in a precise fashion. Using vague language may lead to a misunderstanding. Giving someone directions by telling them that they have to go down the road "about a mile, and then make a left" is not going to get them where they want to go. The operative word is "about", and it tells us next to nothing in terms of arriving at a particular destination. What does "about" mean? *Less* than a mile? *Exactly* a mile? a *little over* a mile? It would make more sense to tell the person that they were to continue on the street they were on for 1.3 miles until they saw a Sonoco station on their left, and then turn left onto Scotland Hill Road. Imagine trying to explain preparing a beef stew by saying that you use a pinch of salt, a smidgen of paprika, and a lot of gravy. The chance that the meal will be as good as you imagined is slight.

Exercise - Using verbal communication only, describe the following to a group of people using language that is clear and precise.
1. How to bake a double chocolate cake
2. How to get to your house from the Garden State parkway.
3. Your choice

Explain, with the aid of a diagram, the following:
1. The nervous system
2. The brain
3. Your choice

Semantics

Semantics is the study of how different words, sentences, and phrases can have the same meaning even though different words are used to describe them. Telling someone that they're great is pretty much the same as telling them that they're fabulous, wonderful, and unbelievable. It's simply a matter of personal choice. Sometimes, words that are used reflect the specific area that you live, and for this reason, misunderstandings may occur. As an example, in the Northeast, we call a particular ice cream topping sprinkles, whereas in the Southwest, they're called jimmies. A trolley is the same as a bus, and a train is known as the tube in England. Grandma is the same as Nana; Father is the same as Pop or Dad.

Language Lunacy

Although the above terminology cannot be found in any reputable text on communication skills or language, it is a simple reminder that the English language can drive a normal person crazy. There are certain words that sound exactly alike - regardless of how clearly we pronounce them - but mean totally different things. As an example, we have the word night...we also have the word knight; we have the word desert...we also have the word dessert. The problem with these words that sound alike but have totally different meanings is that once again we are reminded of the importance of clarifying our phrases and sentences so that there is not a lack of understanding. It also becomes important to learn how to *spell* each of the words correctly so as not to confuse them with the other words that sound the same. Are we starting to get confused here? Let's look at a list of some words that sound alike, but mean different things.

Exercise - See how many definitions you know for the words below. If necessary, look them up in the dictionary. Remember, each set sounds the same, but within the context of a phrase or sentence, means something else.

1. aid -aide
2. cents -scents
3. cite - site - sight
4. counsel - council
5. desert - dessert

6. fair - fare
7. flew - flu - flue
8. formerly - formally
9. idle - idol
10. passed - past
11. principal - principle
12. roll - role
13. root - route
14. see - sea
15. stationery - stationary
16. team - teem
17. there - their - they're
18. weather - whether

Barriers in Communication

There are times when communicating with people seems difficult, if not impossible. We usually attribute these problems to others- rarely to ourselves. Each of us feels that we are effective speakers able to explain our feelings, understand the needs of others, and deal with conflict. Examining the possible barriers may help in explaining potential problem areas:

Polarization comes about when we see things, or analyze them, in extremes. Everything is either black or white with no shades of grey. Someone is either right or wrong, pretty or ugly, wonderful or terrible.

Facts vs.Inferences have already been discussed.A fact is something that has been proven to be true either through scientific data or observation; an inference is an educated guess which may or may not be true.

Allness is the tendency to assume that you know everything there is to know about a particular area, or that what has been said is all there is to say.

Bypassing occurs when the speakers meaning goes over the listeners head. An example of this would be the movie advertisement stating that "absolutely no one will be seated during the last fifteen minutes of the movie", and assuming that this meant that everyone in the theater had to stand for the last part of the film!

Stereotyping occurs when people are "clumped" together in categories, rather than looking at them as individuals with unique traits and talents. One telling sign that a person has the tendency to stereotype is when they use the word "all" to explain something about an individual. Some examples of this would be to say: "all fat people lack will-power," or "all Irish people drink too much."

Exercise - See if you can think of some stereotypical statements of your own. Remember: using the word "all" is the key.

Language Goals

To consider ourselves effective verbal communicators, we must realize that it involves more than using language skillfully, or following the rules of grammar correctly. We must take many other factors into account. The following language goals should suffice as a reminder of our interpersonal responsibilities.

1. Avoid stereotyping - remember that each of us is unique.
2. Avoid the tendency to polarize - there are areas that fall in-between black and white - there is a middle ground.
3. Be a critical listener and try to distinguish between fact and inference.
4. Try to make each of your messages clear; ambiguity will invariably lead to problems and misunderstandings.
5. Avoid language that is racist or sexist.
6. Understand the difference between the denotative and connotative meanings of words.
7. Don't assume you know everything about a topic, or person, or thing. There's always something new to be learned.
8. Don't be afraid to ask questions when meanings are in doubt.

Chapter 7

Voice and Speech
"Is How I Uh, Say, What I Say, Um, Important?"

The average person probably thinks that the words "voice" and "speech" are synonyms - that they mean the same thing. This, however, is not the case. Voice refers to the properties of sound, whereas speech refers to the properties of articulation (clarity - the actual shaping of those sounds). People automatically assume that since they have spent a lifetime speaking, it is something that they do automatically, and do very well. How many times have you spoken to someone, only to have them respond with a "huh," "what did you say?," "could you repeat that please...I didn't understand you?." These are but a few of the common responses that people make when the speaker is unclear. Therefore, it would appear that the problem lies in the fact that we take our voice and speech for granted. Let's analyze some errors:

Case A- Say each of the following statements to a partner :
1. Whatcha doin?
2. When dya think yuz goin?
3. Layduh, ahl go witcha.
4. Godda go!
5. Nah

Case B- Let's say the same thing, a little differently:
1. I would like to enquire as to what your particular plans are at this time?
2. I was sitting here pondering as to when you were thinking of getting ready to leave for your daily activities?
3. At the present time, I have some pressing things to attend to,

but I would like you to keep in mind that I would very much enjoy meeting you later in the day.
4. I am faced with the uncomfortable dilemma of needing to hasten my steps, and depart at this particular time.
5. Negative.

In both cases, all five statements were distorted in one way or another. In Case A, the words were not actually words at all, but combinations of sounds with only a similarity to words. Although not that difficult to figure out, the slurred sounds lack clarity, and may be misunderstood. In Case B, the sentences were so wordy, and overstated, that the language itself becomes distorted, as well as making the listener want to tune out altogether.

Voice

When someone calls you on the phone, can you easily distinguish who the speaker is just by listening to their voice? Most people would answer that depending on how well they know the caller, they would be able to figure out who that person is. We have learned to pick up certain cues from the sound of people's voices that help us determine their mood. We can usually tell if they are excited, angry, depressed, or tired. So then, what exactly is voice? Voice can be defined as: 1.The way one breathes while speaking (**respiration**), 2. How and where the speech sound is created (**phonation**), and 3. The enrichment of the quality of the basic sound (**resonation**). The human voice is similar to that of a violin. In a sense, a violin "breathes" from the opening at its center; similarly, we breathe through our lungs. The violin produces sound by having its strings plucked, creating vibration; similarly, our vocal cords strike one another (like plucking), creating the vibration of sound when we speak. The violin has a rich tone which is created and enhanced by the shape of the instrument, as well as the quality of the wood; similarly, the human voice is enriched by our lungs, chest cavity, bones, nose, mouth, and head.

Respiration

Respiration is the flow of air from the lungs. The air going into the lungs is called **inhalation,** and the air being expelled from the lungs is called **exhalation.** Each time we breathe in, our chest cavity increases and air rushes into the lungs equalizing the pressure with the outside air. When we breathe out, the chest cavity relaxes and becomes smaller in size as the air is released either through the nose (nasal cavity), or the mouth (oral cavity). In order to increase power, we need to learn proper diaphragmatic breathing.

It is always interesting to watch a young child when you ask them to breathe in deeply. Usually, their upper chest will jut out, and their shoulders will rise. Unfortunately, many adults react the same way. They automatically assume that upper chest movement (where the lungs are located) will produce the deepest breath. Any good singer or musician knows from countless hours of practice that proper breathing stems from the diaphragm. **Diaphragmatic breathing** involves the abdomen - not the chest cavity. The best way to determine whether or not you are breathing correctly is to lie down and place a book on your stomach. If you find that the book rises and falls as you breathe in and out, then you are breathing correctly; if you find that the book doesn't actually move at all, then you're doing something wrong. Since breathing is one of those things that come naturally to us during the course of our lives, we spend little, if no time at all, thinking about it. This is where the problem arises in terms of the proper utilization of our voices. Without proper breathing, a myriad of problems may occur: If our intake of breath (inhalation) is not powerful enough, we will be unable to sustain the proper flow of sound. This, in turn, will make our words sound choppy (taking extra little breaths when they are unnecessary), and weak (lacking energy). It should also be mentioned that improper breathing, and lack of breath control, may lead to misunderstandings, and vocal distractions. Speakers who run out of breath tend to distort sounds, and lose the ends of their sentences. They get lower and lower, until little can be heard or understood at all.

People may not realize that when they are nervous, anxious, or tense, their voice is effected. Try to think of the last time you were nervous - possibly before an interview for a job, or before you participated in some sporting event. Do you remember how fast your heart was racing; almost as if you were out of breath from running a great distance? That "out of breath" feeling creates more tension which will ultimately be reflected in your voice. The following are a few exercises to help decrease the tension, and promote better breathing.

1. Select an appropriate posture; make sure that you're comfortable. Your weight should be evenly distributed. Place one foot slightly in front of the other so that you don't look too rigid.

2. Try to alleviate some stress by jogging in place. Nothing too strenuous; just enough movement to loosen up a bit. After a minute or so, add some gentle arm swings.

3. Try releasing tension with a spine roll. Begin in a standing position; lower your chin to your chest, then keep bending to your waist, and finally bend your knees so that your hands are dangling near the floor.

4. Facial muscles may be relaxed by yawning a number of times, and by slow rotations of the head.

Consider the following exercises to help breathe properly while speaking:

1. Inhale deeply using diaphragmatic breathing. Exhale the air slowly by saying "ah". Allow all of the breath to leave your body. Determine how long you were able to make the sound before running out of breath completely. (ten seconds? thirty? a minute?)

2. Inhale deeply once again. Now see if you can count from one to ten slowly on the exhaled air. Was your voice as strong on number ten as it was on number four or five?

3. One more time... inhale deeply. On the exhaled air, state your name, address, and phone number. Were you able to do this comfortably?

4. At home, select a poem, or part of one (approximately eight lines). Practice reading the poem aloud using one breath. Try to listen critically to yourself and determine whether your voice sounds strained in any way, and whether the words are clear.

It was mentioned earlier that poor breathing techniques effect the flow of words. Many people breathe at the wrong time- cutting sentences in the wrong place, creating a lack of continuity, and producing a "choppy" sound. Of course, it's also possible that the reason for the choppy, incorrect, sound is simply a lack of concern or understanding in terms of where the pause ought to be.

Practice the following sentences in terms of both proper breathing, and correct pauses. Remember - think before you speak.

1. According to his resume, he held a steady job for twelve years, and comes to us highly recommended.

2. My friend Carole is a firm believer that top-notch service in a department store is of the utmost importance.

3. Although John originally applied for an executive position at Washout Unlimited, he said he would definitely consider another

position, if it was offered. He did make it clear however that he felt he could easily handle the job as assistant supervisor.

4. You say you're my friend? As the old saying goes, with friends like you, I don't need any enemies.

5. You never really know what the caller really wants, so I learned a long time ago to just get it over with, and return calls as soon as possible.

Phonation

Phonation is the production of sound which is made as the vocal cords come together. All sounds begin in the voice box (larynx) when these two rubberband-like, parallel cords, strike each other. Once again, we can make an analogy to the violin. When you pluck one of the strings of a violin, vibration creates a sound. Unlike the violin however, human vocal cords are small and elastic. In the average woman, these parallel bands are approximately one half to one inch long, whereas in men, they range from three quarters of an inch, to one and one quarter inches long. The length, thickness, and tension of these vocal cords determine a person's **pitch** (the relative high/low sound). For this reason, a man's thicker, longer, vocal cords will ultimately produce a lower sound than that of most women whose vocal cords are thinner and shorter.

There are many times that we tend to abuse our voices. This is particularly true when we scream, laugh too heartily, or find ourselves in a situation where we are trying to speak above other loud noises (at a party, or in a bar). When this happens, our voices become hoarse and harsh sounding. The vocal cords are surrounded by a mucous membrane which acts as a natural protectant, but during those times that we continually strain our voices, the membrane no longer acts as a shield, and we get that grainy, dry, sometimes painful feeling, in our throats.

The following exercises may help you to avoid this hoarseness, and feel more comfortable when you speak:

1. Practice counting from 1-8 with your voice at its lowest comfortable pitch level. Repeat the same thing raising your pitch level slightly. Remember - don't sing the sounds, speak them. After you've done this four or five times, analyze which of the pitch levels was most comfortable for you. This will be fairly easy to detect since you will feel greater tension in your throat if the pitch level you are using is inappropriate.

2. Using the same idea of raising the pitch as you go along,

(starting low and getting higher), say the following sentences aloud:

   a. Up, up, and away, my big balloon - higher - higher!
   b. I just can't believe this. We're on the 103rd floor!.
   c. Let's pick some apples off the tree - reach, stretch, and grab!
   d. Look, up in the sky. It's a bird, it's a plane...it's Superman!

   3. Try starting each of the following statements with a high pitch, and ending with a lower one:

   a. The window washer moved down from the 29th floor.
   b. The childrens blocks came falling, tumbling, crashing down.
   c. Bend slowly from the waist - further, further, lower, lower.
   d. The walls, oh the walls of Jericho came tumbling down.

   4. Listen critically to yourself, or to a partner, as you say the following words. Focus in on the different pitch levels within each one. You'll notice that depending on the word, sometimes you will begin with a higher pitch; sometimes a lower one:

a. blazes	f. condone	k. dim
b. amaze	g. complain	l. behave
c. lantern	h. alarm	m. everyone
d. Indian	i. mimic	n. mountain
e. insane	j. caveman	o. cheers

Resonation

Resonation can be defined as giving sound its distinctive, rich quality. After sound is originated in our larynx, it moves upward towards our mouth. It is at this stage that the richness, or the quality, of the sound is created. If you were to say the sound "ah" leaving a very small opening in the mouth area, how do you think that sound would come out? Would it be rich, hearty, and penetrating? Doubtful. Chances are, the sound would be thin, listless, and weak. Proper resonation begins with the correct use of our oral cavity (the mouth). It is important to practice, and be aware of, the proper size and shape of our mouths when we speak.

   For the most part, the vowel sounds used in Standard American English are pleasing to the ear (a,e,i,o,u). The consonant sounds are not as pleasant -they tend to be more strident and noisy. Since the vowel sounds are the ones that are more "open", they are the ones that can be more easily improved upon by just learning to open the mouth sufficiently, and lowering the jaw. This in turn will help to create a larger cavity for the sound to come out, and a more full-bodied sound to listen to. Depending on the individual, failure to resonate properly will cause different problems. For some, the sounds they make will be tense and throaty; for others, weak and thin. In many other cases, the sounds will be nasal - as if the person was speaking directly through their nose.

To help achieve a pleasing, resonant voice, we need to work on the formation and amplification of our vowel sounds. Simplified, this means that we need to make those sounds the most important ones we make - they must be the ones that are the best supported, and the most prolonged. For practice, say the following words aloud, remembering to prolong the vowel sounds in each.

1. moon	6. thunder	11. zig-zag
2. June	7. fume	12. supreme
3. gold	8. glow	13. approve
4. surf	9. bell	14. open
5. soon	10. sneeze	15. whose

Now practice saying the following phrases by using the vowel sounds to their greatest advantage. (Open your mouth wider than you usually would, and drop that jaw!)

1. You are a sly fox indeed.
2. That's the grand old opera you'll be attending.
3. We'll be going home after Christmas.
4. The morning storm passed quickly over the horizon.
5. The rain in Spain stays mainly on the plane.

Vocal Variety

Vocal Variety can be defined as using your voice to best express the meaning of a message. It is, in a sense, presenting your remarks with flair and color. No one really wants to listen to a person who has a dull, lifeless, voice. Without some emotion behind the words, one's level of interest decreases radically. The tools that are used to help create an interesting, sometimes exciting, voice are **volume, pitch, duration,** and **quality.**

Volume refers to the loudness and softness of your voice. Depending on the size of one's audience, an appropriate volume must be considered. Common sense dictates that if you are a member of a small group, you will not have to concern yourself with speaking very loud. If, however, you are addressing a large group, possibly in an auditorium, you would have to adjust your voice in terms of the volume. Unfortunately, many people assume that if you do not speak "loud and clear," you are simply insecure, or lacking knowledge. Although this may not be the case, it is an assumption that is made very often.

Let us imagine the average student in a speech class. Everyone knows and understands how difficult it is to get up in front of a group of strangers and speak. The student who is talking may find that he/she is sweating, or freezing; frozen like a statue, or shaking uncontrollably; breathing heavily, or barely taking in any air at all. In terms of his or her volume,this student may take a nice deep breath at the outset, and find that by the end of each sentence they are out of breath and inaudible (too low to be heard). This phenomenon is more than likely due to improper breathing techniques, but unfortunately also leads to losing the ends of sentences/thoughts. It's important to remember that what you have to say at the end of each sentence is probably just as important as what you are saying at the beginning, so keep up that volume.

Pitch refers to the high and low levels of your voice. Women usually have higher pitched voices than do their male counterparts, although there are certainly many exceptions here. Michael Jackson is a perfect example of a grown male with a high pitched voice. Regardless of whether you are a male or a female, utilizing pitch to its greatest advantage helps make a speaker more interesting to listen to. Nobody wants to listen to someone speak in a **monotone** (one level tone with no highs or lows). If English is a second or third language for an individual, it is interesting to note that this non-native pitch will be consistent with that of his/her first language.

Duration refers to how fast or slow you speak (rate). There are many reasons why people speak either too fast or too slow, and this depends on their personality as well as the actual speaking situation. In a public speaking situation, saying between 75-125 words per minute is considered best. Since no sane person actually counts the words they speak, it should be understood that this is simply considered to be the average. When someone is happy or excited, they have a tendency to speak too quickly; when they are unhappy or depressed, the tendency will be towards speaking slowly, and deliberately. If you are one of the countless millions who speak too quickly, the best thing to do is to focus in on your related pauses. As an example, let's assume that you ask a friend to pick up some items at the supermarket for you. Chances are, you will be able to quickly list the things that you need, but will the listener be able to understand, and retain the information as quickly? Probably not. It would be best to pause between each item, allowing the listener to absorb and remember what you've said. Slowing down and pausing at appropriate times will also alleviate the problem of repeating words uneccessarily, and using **fillers.**(saying things like "um," "uh," "mm.")

Quality refers to the overall tone of your voice - whether it sounds pleasant, or unpleasant; nasal, or rounded; high -pitched, or broad-ranged. The techniques discussed earlier in this chapter regarding proper respiration, phonation, and resonation, will aid in working towards an appropriate, pleasant, vocal quality.

Vocal Exercises

Look at the following statements, and say each one aloud. Remember to focus in on your volume, pitch, duration, and quality.

1. You're an idiot, a moron, you're dense, and you're stupid.
2. Everyone should be as lucky as I am; I'm rich, and pretty.
3. Do you realize that you're always the first to start trouble?
4. You are a total disgrace to your family and friends.
5. I know you know you'll wind up on the street.
6. You can just forget about getting any allowance this year.
7. Try, just once, to put yourself in his place.
8. In your own quiet way, you're really quite interesting.
9. I know it's difficult, but attempt to be a friend to someone.
10. Is it possible that I'm beginning to hate you?
11. I never win. That's for everyone else on the planet.
12. I'm so excited, I can barely think straight.
13. That show was so boring, I found myself dozing off.
14. Settle down, keep quiet, and live another day.
15. Now you see it, now you don't.
16. I was born here, raised here, and I'll die here.
17. Do you know what you're talking about? I doubt it.
18. How many times do I have to tell you... I don't know.
19. What I say is what I mean. Get it? Got it? Good.
20. He's happy. She's happy. They're all happy.

Speech

When we talk about speech, what we are actually dealing with is the articulation of the particular sounds that we make. **Articulation** is the clear pronunciation of those sounds. Since creating and pronouncing words *seems* to come naturally to most of us, we have a tendency to become sloppy on many occasions. There are times when this is not a problem at all, but other times when it is. Although there are only 26 letters in the alphabet, there are many more sounds that are created from these letters. The sounds can be divided into particular categories:

Vowel sounds - These are sounds that need to be made with an open mouth. The sounds flow, and can be held, or extended, for a long period of time. The basic vowel sounds consist of the letters A,E,I,O, and U, as well as a few combinations of these sounds. The following words contain examples of some of the vowel sounds (underlined):
1. hat, tall
2. help, he
3. will, sit
4. hot, blot
5. who, should

Consonant sounds - These are sounds that are made by diverting or obstructing the flow of air from the lungs. Put simply, consonants are shorter, and more "explosive" sounding than the vowel sounds. The following words contain examples of consonant sounds:
1. put, bring, many
2. time, bid, deal, look
3. crime, bike, grease
4. view, funny, cave
5. zoo, pleasure, going
6. that, three

Diphthong sounds - These are " gliding" vowel sounds. If you were to listen critically, you would notice that the sound made changes as it is spoken within the context of a word:
1. like - the sound changes from an "ah" to an "ee"
2. how - the sound changes from an "aa" to an "oo"
3. usual - the sound changes from an "ee" to an "oo"

4. t<u>oy</u> - the sound changes from an "aw" to an "ee

Articulators - We use one or more articulators to form each of the sounds that we make. These articulators are the **lips, tongue, teeth, hard palate, and soft palate.** Try to determine from the underlined sounds in the following words which articulators should be used in order to pronounce each correctly:

1. <u>f</u>ast
2. par<u>t</u>
3. bra<u>ve</u>
4. <u>th</u>is
5. <u>c</u>rying
6. bri<u>ng</u>
7. <u>th</u>row
8. boar<u>d</u>
9. <u>l</u>ast
10. <u>m</u>any

It is interesting that depending on which part of the country you come from, the actual pronunciation of words, or the sounds within those words, will vary. As an example, in New York and New Jersey, the consonant sound "r" is not always pronounced clearly. Instead of "park", some of us say "pahwk"; instead of "car", we may say "caw". In Massachusetts, the same words would be pronounced "pack" and "caaa". These subtle changes are known as **regionalisms.** Vowel sounds may also vary from region to region. The word "talk" is usually pronounced "tawk" in the metropolitan area, but sounds more like "tock" in the Midwest.

Speech Behaviors

1. **Substitutions** - These refer to *replacing a sound* in a word with another, inappropriate sound.
   a. substituting the "d" sound for the "th" sound -
      <u>th</u>is becomes <u>d</u>is
      <u>th</u>ose becomes <u>d</u>ose
      <u>th</u>em becomes <u>d</u>em

   b. substituting the "d" sound for the "t" sound -
      wa<u>t</u>er becomes wa<u>d</u>er
      li<u>tt</u>le becomes li<u>dd</u>le
      be<u>tt</u>er becomes be<u>dd</u>er

   c. substituting the "n" sound for the "ng" sound -
      runni<u>ng</u> becomes runni<u>n</u>
      parki<u>ng</u> becomes parki<u>n</u>

dancing becomes dancin

d. substituting the "a" sound for the "er" sound -
    later becomes lata
    mother becomes motha
    bother becomes botha

2. **Omissions** - These refer to sounds that are *left out* of a word, when they should be left in.
a. " I'm gonna go tada movies," instead of "I'm going to go to the movies."
b. "She gotta be kiddin," instead of "She's got to be kidding."
c. "You don't know whatcha talkin about," instead of "You don't know what you're talking about."

3 . **Additions** - These refer to sounds that are *added to* a word when they don't belong there.
a. idea becomes idear
b. soda becomes soder
c. wash becomes warsh

4. **Distortions** - These refer to sounds that actually *change the word* altogether.
a. soil becomes serl
b. boil becomes berl
c. toilet becomes terlit
d. film becomes filim

Remembuh - we kin awl sound alot bedda iv we just tink buhfaw we tawk; 1. breed right, 2. make owa sounds loud n cleah, and 3. be aware of awl duh possible substitutions, omissions, additions, and distortions. Keep dese tings in mind, and you'll be poifict!

Chapter 8

Public Speaking Situations
"Can I Capture the Crowd?"

Most people do not like getting up to speak in front of others. It's embarrassing, uncomfortable, and brings on feelings of terrible insecurity. Since few of us can pinpoint what it is precisely that causes our fear of public speaking, the best we can do is settle for some painless remedies to overcome that fear. The more you know and understand, the easier the public speaking experience will be.

The Initial Problems

1. <u>Fear of being judged</u> - Many people fear the public speaking situation because they do not want other people picking apart or analyzing their feelings or beliefs.

2. <u>Fear of failure</u> - Getting up and speaking is one thing; it's quite another when you feel (or know for sure) that you've done a miserable job.

3. <u>Fear of inadequacy</u> - Each of us feels smart in some areas, and not terribly knowledgeable in others. It's not a particularly comforting thought to sense that other people are smarter than you are in the area that you choose to speak about.

4. <u>Fear of negative past experiences</u> - Part of the reason that people don't enjoy the public speaking situation stems from early childhood experiences. If you were ever laughed at, ridiculed, or made uncomfortable about the way you spoke, or how you looked, or how you handled yourself, there's a better than even possibility that you will not want to take the chance of subjecting yourself to that type of situation again.

5. <u>Fear of the unknown</u> - You feel a little uncomfortable; you don't know what to expect? It's at times like this when you know for certain that whatever *can* go wrong, *will* go wrong.

Public Speaking Preparation

The better prepared you are beforehand, the better your presentation will be. Many people assume (incorrectly) that speaking is such a natural process that it should just flow without much thought. This type of thinking can be a major problem when considering how much really needs to be done to ensure some measure of success. Use the following information as a guideline to set yourself up correctly.

1. Choose a topic that you find interesting- perhaps something that you have prior knowledge about. It is important to consider your audience in terms of what they would like to hear, but your choice must ultimately be based on what you are enthusiastic about. A lack of enthusiasm will rub off on your listeners, and their level of interest will be low. If you are speaking about an issue/topic that has been chosen for you, try to find something about the area that interests you enough to convey an element of excitement.

2. Research the topic - Assuming you have chosen something that interests you, or found some element of the issue that you personally find noteworthy, it will be necessary to get substantiating backup material. Regardless of how much you may know about the topic, relying on, and fully utilizing other sources will add a great deal to your presentation. The material may come from books, journals, magazines, newspaper articles, pamphlets, and any other literature you can gather.

3. Formulate and develop your main ideas - One of the biggest problems for the beginning public speaker is the inability to speak for any length of time. One of the reasons for this is a lack of "idea" material. If you've only considered, or prepared, one basic premise or thought for your speech, you're not going to have much to talk about. Brainstorming becomes crucial here- looking at the main issue from different angles, generating new questions from original ideas, and building on each thought.

4. Support the main ideas - If you are presenting an informative speech, your support means defining, describing, or illustrating the concepts that you are discussing. In terms of the persuasive speech, support means proof; turning to reliable source material to show scientifically, historically, or statistically, why you are correct in your thinking or your analysis.

5. Organize the material - One of the easiest ways to lose the attention of your audience is to baffle them with facts that seem to

come out of left field. Decide before you get up to speak how you are going to arrange the material that you have gathered. Once you make a point - stick to it, and present all your information before moving on to the next area. You may want to repeat some major points in the conclusion of your speech, both as a reminder of your purpose, and as a summary.

      6. <u>Word it well; articulate it well</u> - Don't try to impress your audience with big words that few people understand. They may think that you're intelligent, and well read, but they may just as easily feel that you're a pompous phony. The best speakers are the ones who speak *to* their listeners, not *at* them, or *above* them. Use words that are clear, concise, and easily understandable. Try to remember that the clear pronunciation of the words you speak is a critical factor in your presentation. Garbled words will lead to misunderstandings, and ultimately a lack of interest on the part of your audience.

The Informative Speech

      Any time you communicate information, you are telling your listeners something that they did not know before, or shedding light on some new, interesting point regarding the subject. This information is usually presented in one of three ways: **describing**, **demonstrating**, or **defining**. You may decide to incorporate all three into your speech, or two of them, depending on your goal.

      The Descriptive Speech - The speech of description is used when you want to explain something about a person, event, or object. The following are some examples of descriptive speeches:

* The life of our first President - George Washington
* Get ready; set; go - preparing for the Macy's Day Parade
* The last days of the Civil War
* Michael Jackson - the formative years
* The parts of a computer
* The St. Valentine's Day Massacre
* The history of the soap opera
* John F. Kennedy - the assassination
* Vlad the Impaler - A Dracula for all seasons
* The Native American tribes of Bergen County
* An American hero - Jonas Salk
* The unsinkable ship - Titanic

The Demonstration Speech - In this type of speech, the speaker shows how to do or make something. Some examples of a demonstration speech are:

* How to trim that waistline
* How to rollerblade
* How to give yourself the perfect manicure
* You and your VCR - you can learn to operate it successfully
* Baking a pie - the old fashioned way
* Interested in saving a life? - The Heimlich maneuver
* How to change a tire
* Let's make something beautiful - the art of origami
* Keep that great looking smile- brush your teeth correctly

The Speech of Definition - The speech of definition is usually given when the speaker wants to explain - in detail - a difficult concept or idea. The following are some examples:

* Hinduism: The beliefs and customs
* AIDS and cancer - what are the similarities?
* Stocks vs. bonds; which one to choose
* Claustrophobia - panic in a small space
* What is euthanasia?
* The jihad - worth dying for?

Exercise - On a piece of paper, see how many examples of topics you can come up with for the descriptive speech, the demonstration speech, and the speech of definition.

Where to get your material

Once you have decided on a topic, the next logical step is to look for the best available material on that subject area.

1. Your knowledge- If you are a stamp collector, and have decided to present a speech about that, you probably have a lot of information at your disposal already. The fact that you have the coins in your possession and are able to show them, discuss their cost, comment on their worth, talk about how you purchased them - that's a speech within itself. Choosing any topic with knowledge of your own is always a good place to start. You know about it, care about it, and have a measure of experience regarding the area.

2. Interviewing - Speaking to someone who has firsthand

knowledge about your area is a great help. If you decided to speak about AIDS in terms of the psychological effect it has on its victims, imagine how much more powerful it would be if you were able to speak with someone who had the disease; if they were willing to share their feelings as well as their ordeal with you. This type of firsthand knowledge is crucial, and would help make your speech stronger, as well as more believable.

3. <u>Observation</u> - Are you interested in losing weight? Would you like to do it while building good muscle tone so that you look and feel great at the same time? There are many books and articles that can teach you about various weight loss programs, as well as toning and building muscle, but your going to a weight loss center, or observing what goes on in a gym will show you more than any book or article can. When you observe something, you are looking at it yourself - through your own eyes, which will add a personal dimension to your presentation as well as making it more interesting to listen to.

4. <u>Research</u> - Personal knowledge, interviewing, and your own observations are excellent sources. There are times however, when the best information will come from written material.

* Books - If you need to prove a specific point, or present variations of a difficult concept, books are your most valuable tool. They will provide you with the largest, most comprehensive material on any given subject area.

* Encyclopedias - A good place to consider beginning your research. Although not terribly specific or comprehensive, encyclopedias will provide a general idea about many different topics. Be aware of the fact that some of the material you need may not be readily available from this source. As an example, if you are looking for some general information about AIDS, you will not find it in any encyclopedia dated before the 1980s.

* Newspapers - Depending on your topic, a newspaper will afford you the most up-to-date, daily information.

* Periodicals - Publications that come out on a weekly, monthly, or yearly basis, such as Newsweek, Time, or Money Magazine.

The Persuasive Speech

Do you believe that we have been visited by aliens from other worlds? Do you believe in the death penalty? Do you feel that abortion should be legalized? These are tough questions - made more difficult by the fact that people have so many reasons for

disagreeing with each others answers. Compounding this difficulty
is the belief that in many cases, *our* way of thinking is the *rightt*
way of thinking. With this in mind, it stands to reason that
persuading someone to see your side of an issue is not an easy task.

In part, choosing a topic for your persuasive speech should be
based on strong feelings that you have about the issue.If you don't
believe in what you are saying, there's a good possibility that your
listeners won't believe you either. Although it is true that the
experienced lawyer may say one thing in a courtroom, while
believing something else entirely, the beginning public speaker may
not be able to carry this off -at least not at the outset. Another factor
in choosing a topic is the availability of material. Hopefully, with
the numerous choices mentioned previously, you will find what is
needed to prove your point. Keep in mind that for the persuasive
speech, relying on your own feelings and experiences will not be
enough to convince your listeners to see things your way. You will
have to use quotes, statistics, and verifiable facts to help you.

The Proposition

The **proposition** is your goal - it is the statement that you use
to let your audience know what it is that you want them to believe or
do. In terms of the persuasive speech, the speaker will set forth one
of two types of propositions: one of belief, or one of action.

Examples of a **proposition of belief:**

1. I want my audience to believe that there are ghosts.
2. I want my audience to believe that the death penalty is both
   fair and just.
3. I want my audience to believe that state lotteries hurt more
   people than actually help them.
4. I want my audience to believe that euthanasia (mercy-killing)
   is murder.

Examples of a **proposition of action:**

1. I feel that each of us should exercise - for our minds as well
   as our bodies.
2. I feel that all people should be vegetarians - we should
   stop eating meat as well as other animal products.
3. I feel that people with savings accounts should take their

money and invest the funds in stocks and bonds.
4. We should read at least one book a month.

The Introduction, Body and Conclusion of your Speech

"Hi! Today I guess I want to talk to you about how terrible abortion is."Of all the possible introductions, would you consider this to be a strong one? Does this statement reflect any creativity, or thought? The answer to each of these questions is a resounding "NO" In the **introduction,** the speaker should try to capture the audience's attention and interest right from the outset of the speech.This can be done in a number of ways: 1.Tell a story; 2. Make a startling statement;3. Tell a joke (if it's appropriate to the topic);4. Ask a rhetorical question (a question where no response is actually expected); 5. Show a picture; 6. Display a chart; 7. Utilize the blackboard by writing something; 8.Use a quotation;9. Use a piece of poetry. With all these possibilities in mind, can you think of a better introduction for the speech topic mentioned above ?

Exercise - Look at the following topics, and think of a creative way of introducing each of them:
1. Flying saucers - fact or fiction?
2. The homeless - how to get them off the streets
3. Abraham Lincoln - the war years
4. Smoking and lung cancer
5. Charles Manson - man or monster?
6. The sun - friend or foe?
7. Television - a tool for learning, or a boob tube?
8. Martin Luther King - a man with a dream

The **body** of your speech is where the speaker presents his or her basic idea, secondary points, and supporting material to give the statements **credibility.** There's nothing wrong with stating a personal opinion, but they should be backed up by substantiated material such as quotes, statistics, and/or testimonials...these are the things that give the presentation credibility, or believability. If you were to present a speech dealing with the correlation between exposure to the sun and skin cancer, you might decide to startle your audience in the introduction by showing some pictures of people who had skin cancer (remember: sometimes a picture speaks louder than words). You would then explain what you had shown them, why you had shown them what you did, and state your purpose. The bulk of your speech (the body) would follow with various proofs and realities that you had come by through your research. Since the majority of your material will be presented in the body of your speech, it is important that it be well delivered as well as highly organized.

The **conclusion** of your speech serves several purposes. To begin with, you get the opportunity to sum up your main ideas, clarify secondary points, and highlight your beliefs or concerns. As in the case of your introduction, you should carefully consider how you want to end your speech. Remember - your last words can and should leave a strong, lasting impression on your listeners. Saying "Thanks," or "that's it" is passable at best, a cop-out at worst. Once again, you should think in terms of the quote, the picture, the piece of poetry, or the story. Keep in mind that adding humor to a speech is always a good idea as long as it suits the topic, and is not offensive to others.

Exercise - Using the topics mentioned on the previous page, see if you can come up with some ideas for good, solid conclusions. If possible, find a few alternatives.

Choosing a Style of Delivery

After all is said and done, the most lasting impression people are left with after a speech is *how* the speaker presented it. Beautiful words might have been spoken, research might have been impeccable, the speaker might have been brilliant, but if there is no connection with the audience, there is little chance that what was said will make a lasting impact. *What* you say is important, but *how* you say it is just as significant.

Many detractors of Ronald Reagan claimed that one reason he won the election, and was able to sustain a level of credibility throughout his presidency was due to his ability to act - after all, that's what he did for a large part of his career before going into politics. Some of the finest lawyers are consummate actors. They know what to say, when to say it, and how it will achieve the greatest impact; they know when to move, when to be still, when to be overly-emotional , and when to be calm. Similar to the actor and the lawyer, we must realize that "performing" our speech may be the key to achieving many of our speech goals. Remember - we communicate through our bodies (non-verbal communication;

Chapter 9) as well as our voices (Voice and Speech; Chapter 7)

Depending on the particular occasion, your choice of a style of delivery may vary. The four choices available for consideration are: the impromptu, extemporaneous, memorized, and manuscript style.

Impromptu Speaking -Imagine sitting in your speech class and having your teacher ask you to come up in front of the room and talk about your feelings regarding the staggering unemployment rate in this country. Imagine that you have had no time to think about this issue, or plan on what you would say, or necessarily have much to say about it - this would be an impromptu type of speech delivery. It is a speech given on the spur of the moment where you have no time to prepare, or do research, or properly organize the presentation. There are some people who feel very comfortable utilizing this style of speaking. They feel it allows them the freedom to speak their peace without the confines of research or preparation. It is interesting however that the impromptu speech - if successfully presented - will somehow follow the usual rules of the game. The speaker will organize the speech into a semblance of parts; introduction, body, and conclusion. They will consider the verbal as well as non-verbal aspects of the presentation, and for the most part, will have a specific goal in mind.

Exercise - Look at the following statements, and "prepare" an impromptu speech to present in front of the class- you have a minute to do it!
1. What would you do if you won ten million dollars?
2. If you had to spend a year alone on a deserted island and could only bring three books with you, which ones would you choose?
3. Discuss the reasons why college may *not* be for everyone.
4. If we had only one season per year rather than four, which one would you choose.
5. If you knew that you had only one year left to live, what would you do?
6. Do you believe that everyone should wait until they are at least twenty one years old to get married?

Extemporaneous Speaking - The extemporaneous speech delivery is usually the type given in Speech class. It is well thought out in terms of its topic, purpose, and goal; it is well organized, well researched, well delivered, and well rehearsed. Many students neglect this last aspect of their presentation. They assume (incorrectly) that if they've "done the work, and taken some notes," they are ready to get up and speak. This would certainly save some time, but the end result might not be what they had anticipated. Like the actor, any good speaker knows that "practice makes perfect."

The Memorized Speech - Whenever you write out a speech, memorize it word for word, and then present it without the use of any written material, you are delivering a memorized speech. This is probably the most difficult type of speech delivery because very few people are able to remember every single word that they have previously written down. Even those who manage successfully to work it out at home may find that once they get up in front of an audience, they "lose" some the words. Understandably, this could be very embarassing. Imagine that you're in the middle of a crucial statement, your audience is listening attentively, and then - horror of horrors - you can't remember what you're supposed to say next. You stand there, your eyes transfixed on some imaginary page that you can no longer conjure up. Perhaps it isn't worth the trouble spending all that time committing each word to memory. It would seem that working out what you want to say at home with the use of index cards to help keep you organized would probably be a wiser choice. Unless you feel as competent and comfortable as the actor who must memorize their scripts word for word - *don't do it.*. Remember: for the most part, even the actor is able to rely on others to help out if they forget certain words in their script...you have no one but yourself.

The Manuscript Speech - Similar to speaking from memorization, the speaker preparing for a manuscript type of speech delivery writes out the speech in its entirety and then reads it word for word. There are certain occasions when this type of delivery is called for. Among these are topics dealing with foreign policy, trade, business, or a Presidential address. Any occasion where specific language is needed, and making each and every point critical, will find the speaker utilizing this type of delivery. For a manuscript speech to achieve the greatest measure of success, it must be presented with skill. The speaker should read and rehearse the text enough times to create the feeling that the words are flowing from his/her mouth. This preparation will also allow for maximum eye contact since the speaker will know the text well enough to look up often, and establish a measure of rapport with the audience.

Chapter 9

Nonverbal Communication
"Take a guess...What do I mean?"

    Nonverbal Communication is usually referred to as any type of communication without words. There is a sender, there is a receiver, and there is a message - but in this case the message is sent through gestures, movements, artifacts, and paralanguage, rather than through words. Nonverbal communication goes hand in hand with verbal messages; they complement each other. It is the rare individual who speaks without incorporating some type of movement, gesture, or tone to emphasize what they are saying.

    It is a noteworthy fact that many of the immigrants who first came to this country at the turn of the century were unable to speak English. These were people who had no choice but to communicate through body language - and they managed very well. Before explaining the different types of nonverbal communication, let's identify the basic ways that verbal and nonverbal signals interact - the ways, as mentioned earlier - that they go hand in hand:

    To Complement- Nonverbal signals are used to strengthen your verbal messages. If you are telling a friend about the death of a beloved pet, there is a good chance that there may be tears in your eyes at the same time that you are relaying the story. If you're speaking about a funny incident, you may be smiling, or laughing.

    To Substitute - There are quite a few hand signals and gestures that are commonly used which take the place of verbal messages. You can just as easily wave goodbye as say goodbye; you can say "yes," or nod your head to accomplish the same purpose. You can say "I don't know," or shrug your shoulders.

To Repeat - Nonverbal cues are often used to verify whether the listener understands the verbal message. An example of this might be your asking someone to "come here," and then motioning with your head or arm - as if they did not understand what you meant the first time. This is usually done out of habit, and has little to do with the listeners' intelligence.

To Highlight - Nonverbal signals may be used to emphasize a portion of the verbal message. The mother who angrily tells her children to get their toys out of the living room might accompany that request by physically throwing each toy out of the room. This type of behavior usually strengthens, or adds to, the significance of the communication. Saying "I love you" is nice, but is even nicer when followed by a hug or kiss from someone you care about.

To Contradict - There are many instances where someone's verbal message contradicts their nonverbal one. This is usually done intentionally, and the message is easily understood. Telling your brother that you're interested in what he has to say while covering your ears is a sure indication that you're not really interested at all. Crossing your fingers, or winking, indicates to the listener that you're lying or fooling around. There are times when these contradictions are unintentional. You may tell the people involved in the drama club that you're committed to the success of their productions, yet never show up to rehearsals, or come late. You may tell a friend that you can't wait to get together, but never seem to find the time to fit them into your hectic schedule. In essence, you are saying one thing, but actually meaning something quite different. We can see in these instances that "actions speak louder than words." What you show a person in terms of your behavior, and how you act, is a stronger indication of your feelings than anything you might say.

To Regulate - There are times when your nonverbal signals help to regulate your part in the communication process. Raising your hand in class to get the teachers attention, holding your arm out to stop someone from speaking, or tapping a pencil on the desk to show your displeasure, are examples of regulators. These are just a few examples of how you change, modify, or stop the flow of communication.

Kinesics

Kinesics is the study of body language. It is the study of the movements of the head, eyes, arms, and legs, and incorporates all the gestures that are used. It also includes facial expressions which are particularly important since the face is usually the first place someone will look to figure out the true meaning of what is being said. There are numerous occasions where a person says one thing, yet a quick look at their expression tells you that they really mean something else altogether. The face can easily communicate the following emotions: fear, happiness, disgust, anger, sadness, and surprise. Depending on our personalities, some of these emotions can be successfully hidden from others - but not all the time, and not under certain circumstances.

It is interesting that many of our facial expressions are universally shared by everyone. Regardless of language, religion, color, or place of birth, all people display certain emotions- facially- the same throughout the world. You need not understand the person verbally to understand whether they are angry, happy, or disgusted...their expression will be easy to read.

Eye Movements

Most people don't realize that there are certain rules they follow in regard to their eye movements. Unlike certain facial expressions that tend to be universally understood, eye movements will vary depending on the culture. Americans look into the eyes of another for an average of three seconds (gazing). If they look at someone for a longer period of time, it might be construed as showing an unusual amount of interest; if they look at someone for a shorter period, it may indicate a lack of interest in the person, or what that person is saying. It is also considered appropriate to look at the person, and then look away - you never stare for too long a period of time, even if the conversation is a long one. Americans believe that looking into someone's eyes shows that they are not only interested in the conversation, but also honest. Many people believe that averting your gaze means that you have something to hide.

There is a marked difference in the way the Japanese people view eye contact. In many cases, they believe that looking someone straight in the eye shows a lack of breeding and respect. They will look at someone briefly, and then look away.

Pupilometrics is the study of the dilation of the pupils of the eyes. Depending on the mood of the person, their pupils will dilate giving clues as to their particular frame of mind. Pupils dilate (enlarge), when a person is excited, and constrict (get smaller), when someone is angry, or feeling negatively about a situation.

Territoriality

Territoriality refers to the space, or area, that a person feels is his or her own. A perfect example is the classroom situation. If a student is assigned a seat, he or she will take that seat on a daily basis because they are "forced' to do so; but the student that is not assigned a seat will usually choose one for themselves, and take the same one each time they come to class. In a sense, it becomes "their seat." If the seat itself is not available, or if there has been a rearrangement of chairs, the student will still take a seat in the approximate area that they usually sit. Sometimes, there is a specific goal in mind when choosing where a person will sit. You may want to hide out, so you choose an area in the back of the room; you may want to show off your knowledge in a particular class, so you choose to sit front and center. Whatever the case, you choose an area that you feel comfortable in, and claim it as your own.

Choosing- or being given - a specific chair at your kitchen table, picking a favorite living room chair, a particular spot on the couch, or sleeping on a certain side of the bed, are also examples of territoriality. It is perhaps an important human need to feel that certain things "belong" to you.

Markers represent the specific ways that we identify our particular territory:

1. Central markers - We use central markers to reserve an area or territory for ourselves. Examples of central markers are putting a jacket on a chair to let someone know that it's taken, or placing books on a table to signify that the area is in use.

2. Boundary markers - Boundary markers are used to set a barrier between what is your territory, and what is others'. Examples of boundary markers are the armrests on airplanes and movies, or a fence between homes.

3. Ear markers - Ear markers identify personal possessions. Examples of ear markers are monogrammed shirts, nameplates, initials, or names that are placed on coats and luggage.

Proxemics

Proxemics is the study of personal space. Whether you stand very close to someone, allow them to stand close to you, or keep your personal distance, it says something about you, and about your relationship with others. Sometimes, this spatial distance is self-chosen, and sometimes it is dictated by the society in which you live. There is the case of Jeremy who hated to be too close to people. He had a wonderful, loving, and affectionate home life with his wife and daughter, but outside the home he appeared to be a cold, untouchable person. When asked about this, he easily explained that he had spent the better part of his childhood surrounded by five siblings, and nine cousins, who all lived in the same building. Although he loved his family, he said he always felt like he was being "choked." He claimed to feel as if he "never had any space." As an adult, he chose to have only one child, and to live far from the rest of his family -not out of hatred, but out of a need for the space that he lacked as a child.

It is important to keep in mind that this scenario may sound familiar, but depending on the person, the outcome may be different. Many people who have been raised surrounded by large families tend to want the same thing when they are older, and don't mind the closeness, or the lack of "personal space."

Spatial relationships are also culturally dictated. Americans, in general, tend to need more personal space than many people from other countries. If one person speaks too closely to another, it will usually be the American who will back away to provide a little more distance. This happens naturally, and is not usually done as an insult, or as a way to avoid the person.

Spatial Distances

According to Edward Hall, there are four distinct distances that define and determine the nature of relationships between people.

Intimate distance is the distance between people that ranges from touching to approximately 18 inches. This is considered to be very close contact since each person involved can almost feel and smell the others' breath. Lovemaking, fighting, and comforting are examples of intimate distance.

Personal distance ranges from 18 inches to 4 feet from another person. According to Hall, people have an imaginary "bubble" that defines and protects their personal distance. As in the case of Jeremy, each of us determines the distance from others that makes us comfortable. For some of us, 18 inches is more than enough space; for others, 3-4 feet will more likely put us at ease, and make us feel more secure.

Social distance ranges from 4 to 12 feet, and tends to be more formal in terms of the interaction between people. Social distance is usually reserved for business meetings, interviews, and those situations where the people involved are goal oriented.

Public distance ranges from 12 to 25 feet, and gives the person involved plenty of space. If you were presenting a speech in a classroom situation, this would be the approximate space between you and your audience. Of the four types of spatial distances, public distance is the most formal.

Haptics is the study of touch. It is the sense that develops sooner than the others, and considered to be crucial for one's social, emotional, and psychological well-being. As soon as a child is born, he or she is patted, stroked, kissed, hugged, and held. This is important and necessary for the infant whose world revolves around other people, and who get their sense of love and acceptance from the physical world around them.

As in other types of nonverbal communication, the importance of touch will vary from culture to culture. Americans touch each other more than the Japanese, yet not nearly as much as many southern Europeans. Men in France kiss each other openly as a gesture of friendship, or as a way of saying "hello," whereas most American men find this uncomfortable, and less than masculine. The American woman, however, does not feel this to be a particular restriction, and believes that kissing - both men and women - is socially acceptable.

Touch is important, it is necessary, and it conveys many different emotions, as well as having meaning in various situations. We touch one another to show that we care about the other person (putting an arm around them); that we are angry with them (shoving or hitting them); and that we are in control (telling them by touch to move over, stay put, or hurry up).

Artifactual Communication

Artifactual communication are those nonverbal messages that deal with clothing, color, jewelry, and decorative space. Each says something about who we are, and how we feel about the objects around us.

Clothing functions as protection from the elements, covering for modesty's sake, display of our many assets, and the coverage of our less than desirable attributes. Living in a big city allows people the freedom to dress in many eclectic ways. Since there are so many ethnic groups, almost anything goes, and almost anything is considered acceptable. Despite this freedom, there are still a number of conventional restrictions that are placed upon us. Wearing jeans and a tee-shirt to class may be considered appropriate attire, but would not be considered as such in an interview situation. Wearing a low-cut, floor-length gown to a wedding might draw envious stares, but would be looked on with horror if worn to the office.

Whether you consider it fair or not, many people judge others by the way they dress. If a person approached you in tattered, dirty clothes, your probable reaction to them would be to back away for fear that they were beggars, or worse. A well-dressed person, however, is looked at comfortably, and even respectfully, and may not be considered at all dangerous - although they might be. We make inferences about people (judgments not necessarily based on fact), and stick to them due to our own beliefs and prejudices.

Color has many meanings, and affects us in both positive and negative ways. We like some colors, and dislike others; we wear certain colors, and would not dream of wearing others; we paint rooms certain colors, and color- coordinate our furniture, lighting fixtures, and carpeting. Painting a baby's room red seems somehow inappropriate, yet not so for a bordello; painting your kitchen a bright yellow feels right, but it is doubtful that you would paint your living room in the same shade. Colors convey feelings, and moods, and "say" things to others about us:

red - signifies warmth and passion, but also signifies war, death, and the devil.

yellow - signifies happiness and wisdom, but also signifies cruelty of spirit, and cowardice.

blue - signifies truth and devotion, but also signifies sadness and depression.

green - signifies nature and fertility, but also signifies jealousy, envy, and disgrace.

Many people choose colors to wear based solely on what they think suits them. "Specialists" in color coordination will teach you whether you are a "fall" person, or a "winter" person, and help you choose clothing that best complements your skin tone. Heavy people are reminded that bright colors are to be avoided; every good business person knows the strength of navy blue, as compared to the weakness of brown; in our culture, white is usually worn by the bride, but not necessarily by the groom; at funerals, black seems to be the fashion statement- or at least a dark, somber, color to remind us of the seriousness of the occasion.

Jewelry can make many statements about you - some made intentionally, others not. Wearing four gold chains around your neck may signify nothing more than your passion for good jewelry; or it may be an intentional statement regarding your financial worth. A diamond ring worn by a female usually means that she is engaged to be married, and let's the rest of the world know that she is no longer available. A college ring communicates a message, as does any number of buttons worn on jackets or shirts. Nose rings and rings worn through the stomach area communicate different things to different people. Wearing too much jewelry during an interview is not considered appropriate, but is fine at a formal affair. Jewelry worn on the beach may be foolish, or fine, depending on your particular outlook.

Decorative Space has to do with the way you set up your furniture. If you decorate your own home or apartment, much can be said about the type of furniture you have, as well as how, and where, you place individual pieces. Putting chairs around a fireplace indicates one interest, as compared to placing those chairs around the television set. Having bookcases filled with classic literature says something different than scattered magazines lying around the house. Paintings, or other works of art, reveal much about what you like, and what you find important. What you *don't* have says something about you too. An apartment, or home, without any "extras," such as books, television, or radio, may indicate a lack of money to some people, a lack of intelligence and sociability to others, or a sign that the person who lives there is just too busy.

Chronemics

Chronemics is the study of time; how we view it, and it's importance in our everyday lives. Whereas some people place great value on time, there are others who find it an unnecessary burden, stifling their freedom.

There are two basic types of time - *formal, and informal. Formal time* deals with seconds, minutes, hours, days, weeks, months, and years. We all realize that classes meet on a particular day (or days), and at a particular time. Coming late to certain classes will inevitably lead to trouble if the instructor places a great deal of value on punctuality. If you have a court date, it's expected that you will be there at the convenience of the court ...not when it's good for you. Showing up late for your own wedding would probably be considered a broach of etiquette, as would showing up late for a loved one's funeral. Your status in life also determines whether you will be punctual or late. A meeting with your employer calls for punctuality (if you're wise), whereas a meeting with a friend allows a little more freedom. Telling the friend that you were late because you got stuck on the phone is acceptable (sometimes), but using that excuse with your boss sounds immature and foolish.

Informal time refers to general statements such as "quickly," "as soon as possible," "forever," and that old favorite - "never." The reason these words are general, rather than specific, lie in the nature of their meaning. Keep in mind that: " Words don't have meaning, people do." The word "quickly" may indicate a matter of minutes for me, but a matter of hours for you. "Forever" is a tricky word that should not be used as often as it is, because almost nothing lasts forever; and we've all been told, at one time or another, that we should "never say never" - indicating that almost anything is possible.

Look at the following statements, and see whether you are a time-conscious person or not. Indicate for each whether you believe the statement to be true or false.

_____1. If I hand in an assignment a week late, it does not really bother me.

_____2. Showing up at a friend's home on time for dinner is not a great concern.

_____3. I usually plan for my vacations ahead of time by putting money aside each week.

_____4. I care more about tomorrow than I do about today.

_____5. I don't show up on time to most of my classes.

_____6. Showing up late for an appointment with my boss is acceptable because I can always tell him/her that I was busy working.

_____7. I'm usually late for parties.

_____8. I find it difficult to complete projects on time.

_____9. I believe in doing things on the spur of the moment - planning ahead is not nearly as much fun.

_____10. I'm big on making lists so that I don't forget things.

Except for questions 3 and 10, if you answered "true" to most of the statements above, then you are not overly concerned with time, and you might want to reevaluate your priorities. It may be true that your friends and family will accept you as you are - late or not- but the rest of the world may not be quite as understanding.

The importance of time also varies from country to country. There are places - generally in southern climates - where time is looked on in a more relaxed fashion. This may be due in part to the heat, or it may be culturally determined. In the northern climates - Switzerland, as an example - time is almost an art form. When someone talks about having a Swiss watch, one of the first things you think of is "precision timing." A train leaving Geneva, Switzerland at 2:07, leaves at *precisely* that time - not one minute later, not one minute earlier. This can become an expensive proposition if you have paid for a ticket and show up even 30 seconds late. It would be wise to understand beforehand what is expected of you in terms of time, and realize that it is different for different people, in different places, in different situations.

Paralanguage

Paralanguage is the only type of nonverbal communication that can be heard. It is the tone of your voice, and reflects the mood, or feeling, behind the actual words that you use. It is vocal, not verbal, thereby placing it into the category of nonverbal communication. Remember: verbal means words, and we are now discussing the tone associated with those words, rather than the words themselves. Paralanguage is also reflected in our pitch, rate, volume, and rhythm. Every time you ask a question, raise your voice, emphasize a point, or get intentionally sarcastic with someone, you are using your vocal apparatus to surround your words with meaning. Paralanguage is also known as **vocalics** - a different word, but the same meaning.

You may not realize how often you use paralanguage as a substitution for words. An example of this would be your saying "huh?" rather than "what do you mean?". Keep in mind that "huh" is *not* a word; you may use it as part of your everyday vocabulary, but you can't find it in the dictionary - it is a vocalization (a sound), not a verbalization (a word).

Probably the best way to understand the significance of paralanguage in your everyday life is to examine the following statements, and determine how each can have different meanings depending on your paralinguistic cues. Keep in mind that each statement can communicate happiness, praise, pity, criticism, or contempt - it all depends on *how* you say it.

1. I'm really crazy about you.
2. Did you honestly think that I would forget to invite you?
3. Your brother is really something.

4. Funny...I thought you were quite a bit older.
5. That was some dinner.
6. You're the professional.
7. You lost 10 pounds?
8. You got an A in our speech class?
9. I'm amazed at your compassion.
10. She's an incredible teacher.
11. I think I'm going to be sick.
12. I'm happy; I'm really happy about your engagement
13. I would appreciate your leaving this house.
14. They make more money than anyone I know.
15. Hello...I'm over here...do you hear me?

Once you realize that there are any number of ways to "say" something, you should be prepared to analyze your own nonverbal communication patterns. You may think that you are saying one thing, but may actually be coming across another way altogether. You should be willing to change, or modify, some of your nonverbal behaviors, as well as learning to understand the paralinguistic behavior of others. Try to resist the temptation of jumping to conclusions - sometimes your assessment will be correct, but on other occasions, you will be making an error in judgment that will lead to unnecessary communication problems.

Chapter 10

Interviewing Skills
"Can I Have This Job Please?"

Imagine this: You're all dressed up, feeling hot and sweaty and uncomfortable, You're in a busy, midtown Manhattan office surrounded by people who don't look like they're at all interested in being your friend. You're heart is beating so fast, and so loud, that you're fairly certain most of the people around you can hear it. You are very thirsty and you are not quite certain whether your shaking is due to nerves or the beginning of some type of seizure.

You're Waiting To Be Interviewed!

You've gone to school for what seems like an eternity just waiting for this moment. You know that you would be good at this job, if only someone would give you the opportunity to prove it. You know you have to come across the right way and "sell yourself," but how? You realize that you are going to be asked a number of questions, but which ones? You're probably wishing right now that you had a crystal ball so that you would know what to expect, and more importantly, what the outcome would be. Wishing, dreaming and hoping may help you emotionally, but having concrete information about the interviewing process will help you to secure the job more readily.
Remember: If you are well prepared beforehand, then your apprehension will be lessened; your chances of performing well will increase; and the possibility of your getting the job will be greater.
In this chapter we will go over some of the crucial skills that are necessary to your inevitable success in "The Interview Game".

The Interview

According to the Random House dictionary, an interview is "a formal meeting in which a person or persons question, consult, or evaluate another." It is markedly different from other forms of communication in that questions and answers are the norm, rather than the exception. An interview takes place in order for a person (or a number of people) to understand/evaluate the needs, strengths, or weaknesses of another; to learn more about a problem; or to learn about a product. Depending on the specific goal, one or more types of interviews would be beneficial to suit the needs of the interviewer and interviewee.

The Counseling Interview

This is an interview to provide guidance. Everyone needs help once in a while to deal with certain problems in their lives. These problems may involve the working environment, something that is personal, or simply dealing with the day-to-day headaches of living. The interviewer in this type of interview must learn a great deal about the person involved if any benefit is to be derived from the meeting.

The Appraisal Interview

This is also known as the evaluation interview, and can be very helpful to a new employee. The interviewee's performance on the job is assessed by "the boss", or personnel, and is then advised how to improve. In some instances, the person involved may be commended on something that they have accomplished. Whether the appraisal is positive, negative, or a combination of both, the employee will undoubtedly learn more about how they are thought of within the context of the organization.

The Exit Interview

Many large corporations utilize this type of interview when an employee decides to leave the job voluntarily. Due to the very competitive nature of business, it becomes necessary for any employer to understand why an employee would want/have to leave the job. Whether the reason is money, unfair treatment, or a move to a new state, it would undoubtedly help to know the answer.

The Persuasive Interview

The ultimate goal in the persuasive interview is to change a person's behavior, attitudes or beliefs. An example of a persuasive interview would be your going into a store to purchase a washing machine. A simple enough task until you realize that the salesperson wants you to purchase a machine in that particular store. What they don't want you to do is leave and take your business elsewhere. Their goal is to persuade you into believing that the machines they carry are better, prettier, cheaper, and in general, more worthy of your consideration. The better they are at persuading you, the better their chances are of making the sale. The same can be said about purchasing a home. The more persuasive the homeowner, or realtor, the more they can sell you on the glory of the home, thereby enhancing the chance that there will be a sale.

The Informative Interview

In this type of interview, the interviewer is concerned with learning something about the interviewee - usually a famous person. An example would be Oprah Winfrey interviewing Roseanne Barr, and asking questions about her life, marriage and television success. The aim would probably be to get "a scoop;" some new information that would capture the interest of the people watching the show. Hopefully, it would be something that would anger, sadden, fascinate or gladden the hearts and minds of the listening/viewing audience. For those people interested in conducting this type of interview, the following points should be carefully considered:

*Prepare all questions ahead of time. Don't ever assume that ideas will pop into your head at the appropriate moment.
*Don't assume that the person you are interviewing will be talkative, or willing to go into detail about personal or business matters. You - as the interviewer - must be ready with follow-up questions to keep the conversation flowing.
*Establish rapport- Try to learn enough about the person you are interviewing so that they feel comfortable in your presence. Keep in mind that the more at ease they are, the more they will be willing to talk to you - particularly about personal issues.
*Always ask open-ended questions. These are questions that require more than a one word answer. Asking someone, "Are you happy?" may simply get a yes or no response, but phrasing it by

saying "Can you tell me specifically in what particular ways you consider yourself to be a happy person?" paves the way for a more detailed, and probably interesting, response.

*Always remember to express appreciation for their time at the end of the interview, and thank them.

*It would be a good idea to send a letter expressing how wonderful it was to get the opportunity to interview the person. Keep in mind that you may want to interview them again at some time in the future...so be polite!

The Employment Interview

In this type of interview, a great deal of persuasion and information will go back and forth between the interviewer and the interviewee. Of all the types of interviews mentioned thus far, this one is probably the most important one for the graduating student looking to secure employment.

1. Be Prepared Mentally. Learn something about the school, company or organization that you are interviewing for. Be prepared to call for brochures, read the trade papers, and get information from any reliable source. Understand beforehand that you are applying for a specific position. Know what the job description is, what the employer is looking for, and if possible, what you will be expected to do. The more information you have at your disposal before actually going in for the interview, the more comfortable you will be when the time comes for you to answer and ask questions.

2. Be Prepared Physically. The importance of your physical presentation cannot be stressed enough. What you decide to wear, and how you wear it may determine whether a prospective employer will seriously consider you for a position. For a female, a skirt and blouse are always acceptable, but wearing a mini-skirt with a halter might project the wrong image - regardless of how good that person may look in the outfit. A running suit - regardless of how expensive it is -may look as if you did not care enough to dress up for the occasion. There's an easy rule to follow here:

When in doubt, go conservative

* Dress in clothes that are not "faddish". These are usually the ones that are in one year, and out the next. An example of this would be

the micro-mini skirt or bell-bottom pants which appear and
then disappear for a period of time.
* Dress in muted colors rather than loud ones.
* Make sure that clothes are clean and pressed and that the shoes
  you choose to wear are polished/buffed.
* Nails should be manicured, or at least look that way.
* Jewelry should be kept at a minimum, as should the amount of
  perfume or cologne you decide to use.

3. Understand the Objectives of the Interview.
  Considering how important the employment interview is to your
  future, the following guidelines should be followed:
* Know what you want, and what your goals are.
* As mentioned above, dress carefully.
* Arrive on time. The old saying "Better late than never" does not
  apply here.
* Try to remember all you know about good interpersonal skills.
* Since there are certain questions that pop up all the time, have
  answers ready - and be ready to ask some of your own.
* Communicate confidence. It is understood beforehand that you
  will undoubtedly be nervous. This is because you care. Learn to
  control your emotions, and be willing to speak up.
* Re-sell yourself. A thank you note to the interviewer shows
  both your courteous nature, and serves as a reminder of who
  you are - again. The note may not help, but it can't hurt.

4. Interview Barriers
  The most common reasons why people fail to do well during
  interviews are the following:
* They are not prepared to answer questions effectively. There are a
  list of questions which will be discussed later in the chapter that
  can help in this area. Similar to learning the lines in a play,
  anyone can practice answering a number of questions as long as
  they know what will be asked of them.
* They have no pertinent questions to ask. The more information
  one has at their disposal regarding the organization, the more
  likely they will be able to ask intelligent questions which will
  help them, and show the interviewer their enthusiasm.
* They come to the interview with no "back-up" material. They
  have no resume; no school records; no citations, and no letters of
  recommendation.
* They come in with no information at hand regarding the

    organization or the requirements of the job.
* They dress inappropriately and carelessly.
* They are poor listeners who get easily distracted, answer questions incorrectly, and need things repeated.

Interviewing Scenario

Let's look at the following dialogue, and ascertain how the applicant might have fared better than he did.

The Set-Up: Applicant for job at Pompous Publications enters posh office in midtown Manhattan with his friend Paul. After a short wait, he is told that Mrs. Clark is ready to see him. He enters her office, and stands politely at the door waiting to get a cue as to his next move.

The Scene

Ms. Clark: Come in Mr. Kent.

Mr. Kent: Oh, yeah...Thanks.

Ms. Clark: So, Mr. Kent, how are you today?

Mr. Kent: All right, I guess. I have to be honest with you about something. I'm a little nervous.

Ms. Clark: Believe me, I understand completely.

Mr. Kent: You do?

Ms. Clark: Yes, I do. So you're interested in working for us?

Mr. Kent: Well, uh, yeah. I mean, I heard it's a pretty good company to work for.

Ms. Clark: Really. That's nice. Who did you hear this from?

Mr. Kent: I don't remember.

Ms. Clark: Tell me what you know about the publishing business.

Mr. Kent:	Well, I took a number of courses in college.
Ms. Clark:	Can you tell me about some of those courses?
Mr. Kent:	Wow. Well, there were a lot of them.. If you take a look at my transcript, they're all listed there.
Ms. Clark:	(Looking through some papers on her desk) I don't seem to have a copy at my disposal here. Do you by chance have another copy with you?
Mr. Kent:	No. I'm sorry. I honestly didn't think that I would need to bring one along since I had sent you one. I kind of figured you wouldn't lose my stuff.
Ms. Clark:	Oh. In your own words then, what do you know about the publishing business?
Mr. Kent:	Wow. That really is a tough one. You know, I've never worked for a company like this before.
Ms. Clark:	Well. Maybe I can help you there. What would you like to know?
Mr. Kent:	Mmm...Can I have a minute here?
Ms. Clark:	Certainly. Take your time.
Mr. Kent:	(After a few seconds) Well, is it a fifty week work year?
Ms. Clark:	Excuse me?
Mr. Kent:	I mean, do I get two weeks' vacation? or one? or three if I'm like employee of the year?
Ms. Clark:	I can appreciate your concern about vacation time Mr. Kent, but you haven't answered my question.
Mr. Kent:	Oh sorry, what was the question?

Ms. Clark: I asked what information you'd like about the publishing business.

Mr. Kent: Oh, yes. Let me see...well, nothing really, I guess.

Ms. Clark: All right then. Why do you think that I should hire you?

Mr. Kent: Well, I think that I would be the best person for the job because of all my course work in school, and from the job description in the newspaper, I think that I would actually like working here.

Ms. Clark: Do you realize what your particular responsibilities would be if you were to get this position? Do you understand that you would have to accomplish numerous tasks on a daily basis?

Mr. Kent: Well, I assumed that in a company this size, there would be a lot of competent people to help me out.

Ms. Clark: But what are your particular strengths? What would you be bringing to the company?

Mr. Kent: Well, I guess that we're both going to have to find out about that. You know, I'll feel my way through. I'm willing to listen, and I'm certainly willing to learn.

Ms. Clark: That's nice to know. Tell me Mr. Kent...do you always wear those earrings?

Mr. Kent: What, these? (grabbing hold of his ear) Well, yeah, as a matter of fact I do. They're me. I mean, they kind of tell people who I am.

Ms. Clark: And who exactly are you?

Mr. Kent: What? Oh, that's funny!

Ms. Clark: Would you be willing to remove them?

Mr. Kent:	What? Now? Oh, you mean if I got the job? Well, I guess if it meant getting the position or not, sure I would get rid of them. But I wouldn't be happy about it. I mean, like I said before. These earrings are me. They help to establish my identity.
Ms. Clark:	I see. Well, Mr. Kent, is there anything else you have to add, or anything at all that you need to know about the job, or the firm?
Mr. Kent:	Just one more thing. If I do get the job, when would I be expected to begin?. To be honest with you, I had a short vacation planned. You know, a little rest and relaxation before getting down to work.
Ms. Clark:	The person chosen for this particular position would begin in approximately six weeks. Is that a problem?
Mr. Kent:	That's great. I mean, that won't be any problem at all.
Ms. Clark:	I'm so happy to hear that. Is there anything else?
Mr. Kent:	Nope. I think I've said it all.
Ms. Clark:	You certainly have.

Looking at this particular scenario, it is apparent that Mr. Kent was not at all prepared for the interview. He did not know anything about the company; he was ill-prepared to answer any questions; he had no questions prepared to ask of the interviewer, and his basic concern seemed to be his vacation time and when he had to begin the job. Keep in mind that the pre-interview period must begin long before the actual interview takes place. You must be prepared both physically and intellectually, and above all, you must be ready to ask and answer a specific set of questions.

TYPICAL INTERVIEW QUESTIONS

The smart interviewer will be able to answer a number of questions ranging from their educational background to their personal interests. The following list represents a sample questionnaire. Although it is not likely that you will be asked all of these questions, it is uncertain which ones will be asked....therefore, it's wise to know, and be prepared beforehand to answer all of them.

A. Personal Background
1. Tell me a little about yourself.
2. Where do you live?
3. How long have you lived there?
4. What are your favorite hobbies?
5. What do you usually do in your spare time?
6. What things do you think you do best?
7. What are some of the things that you don't like to do?
8. How do you like to spend your vacations?
9. Do you feel that you can work under pressure?
10. Tell me about some community activities that you have participated in within the last year or two.
11. If you get this position, would you be willing to relocate?
12. How great a distance would you be willing to travel in order to get to work? (in miles, or hours)
13. Do you have anything you would like to add about yourself?

B. Education
1. What high school did you attend?
2. Did you graduate from high school? If not, what was the last year of school that you attended?
3. While in high school, did you receive any special training? Were you on any teams?
4. Which courses were your favorites?
5. Which courses did you dislike?
6. Did you participate in any extracurricular activities?
7. What can you tell me about your favorite teacher?
8. Tell me about your education since high school.
9. In college, why did you choose your particular major?
10. Which courses did you like the best?
11. Which courses did you like the least?
12. Now that you're older and wiser, would you do things differently?
13. Do you plan to go on with your education?
14. If you take more courses, which ones would you take?

C. Skills Training
1. Have you attended vocational or technical school?
2. Were there any vocational programs at your high school?
3. Have you had any on-the-job training?
4. What vocational skills do you possess?
5. Can you operate any machinery?
6. Have you developed any vocational skills from hobbies?
7. Tell me about other skills programs that you have become involved with beyond high school.

D. Work or Work Related Experience
1. Have you held any full-time jobs?
2. Have you held any part-time jobs?
3. Tell me about you last job.Did you like it?
4. What duties did you perform on your job?
5. How much money were you making?
6. Did you like your last supervisor?
7. Why did you leave your last job?
8. What can you tell me about your co-workers on your last job? Did you get along with them? If not, why not?
9. What position are you interested in?
10. Did you learn anything important from your last job? If so, could you explain what you learned? If not, do you feel that you learned nothing due to the fact that the job was boring or stagnant?
11. What did you like the most about the last job that you held?
12. What did you like the least about it?
13. What kind of reference do you think your last teacher or supervisor will give you?
14. Why do you feel that you will like doing this job?
15. Where did you hear about this job offering?
16. What are your salary expectations here?
17. Do you prefer to work alone, or with other people?
18. Do you believe that you can effectively perform the duties required on this job?
19. What do you see yourself doing ten years from now?
20. Do you feel that you could be as perfectly satisfied doing the same thing in ten years as what you would be hired for at this time?
21. Do you have any questions ?

E. Vocational Interests

1. What advantages do you think there are to working here?
2. Does this job have any disadvantages as far as you know?
3. What job would you least like to do?
4. In what way do you feel you could benefit this company?
5. How did you become interested in this type of work?
6. Tell me what you know about this company.
7. Briefly explain why you feel qualified for this position.
8. What can you tell me about our products/services?
9. Where did you get your information regarding this company?
10. In what way(s) would your past experiences help you to perform your job here?

Before preparing to answer the job interview questions, review the following checklist:

1. Don't try to memorize your answers. Simply familiarize yourself with the questions that may be asked so that when you speak, you sound both natural and sincere.
2. Try to determine whether you are being asked an open or closed question. Remember, an open question calls for a more detailed response, whereas the closed question is simply asking for a "yes" or "no" response.
3. Be sure to emphasize your strengths.
4. Be aware of your weaknesses without bringing unnecessary attention to them...but don't lie.
5. Keep the open-ended questions to less than two minutes.
6. When asked a closed question (yes or no answer), sound as confident as possible.

THE RESUME

Sending a resume, and bringing one with you at the time of an interview is crucial. The resume should be clear, clean, and well typed with no spelling or grammatical errors. If necessary, the work should be done professionally on a good typewriter or computer. Let's look at a sample resume on the next page as a guideline for preparing one of your own.

ILANA MERRICK
24601 Javert Boulevard
Nanuet, New York 10954
(914) 627-1979

OBJECTIVE
To secure a position as a drama teacher in a high school.

EDUCATION
B.A., Carnegie Mellon, Pittsburgh, Pennsylvania

MAJOR: Theater Arts, with an emphasis on acting and directing.
MINOR: Speech Communication.
Courses included: Acting, Oral Interpretation of Literature, Stage Movement, Directing, History of the Theater, Dance for the Theater, Public Speaking, Interpersonal Communication, Small Group Communication, Persuasive Techniques.

Extra-Curricular Activities: Drama Club (three years), performed in six productions - both dramas and musicals, directed two productions, participated twice in the schools' Speech Competition, (Second place winner and Honorable Mention)

Honors: Graduate Assistantship.

WORK EXPERIENCE
Four summers working with "County Kids," a drama/musical workshop program for children ages 7 - 17: Worked as an assistant to the director and the choreographer.
One year working as a singer with the touring group "Broadway Bound" at various clubs and regional theatres in the tri-state area.

HOBBIES
Enjoy acting, singing, dancing, traveling, reading, and tennis.

REFERENCES
Dr. Peter Cerveris (Carnegie-Mellon) Director:Student Productions
Dr.Tommy Townsend (Carnegie-Mellon) Theater/Music Professor
Prof.Steven Gellicle (Carnegie-Mellon) Chairman: Dept. of English

"ILLEGAL" QUESTIONS

Most people are unaware of the fact that there are a number of questions that might be asked that do not have to be answered. This is a very difficult position to be put in since any well-mannered person would attempt to answer all questions politely, even if they felt uncomfortable doing so. When dealing with a friend, acquaintance, or possibly a relative, you would probably feel both comfortable and justified telling them to mind their own business. This would not however be the case when dealing with a prospective employer. The choice then is yours. It is a personal decision. You can either answer, or refuse - *tactfully*.

* What political organizations to you belong to?
* How tall are you?
* Have you ever been arrested?
* How much do you weigh?
* Do you own your own home?
* Are you married, divorced, separated?
* Do you owe a lot of money on your charge cards?
* Do you consider yourself to be a religious person?
* Do you carry much insurance?
* Are you living with anyone?
* What is your race, religion, national origin? (Illegal in many, although not all states.

The best strategy in handling some, or all of these illegal questions would be to answer those parts of the question that you do not object to, and simply leave out any information that you do not wish to discuss. Keep in mind that if you are comfortable with this type of questioning (undeniably personal), you are free to say whatever you like.

The Do's and Dont's of the Interview Game

As a short summary, let's put everything in a neat pile. Although it's true that you will learn from experience, some specific guidelines in handling the interview situation should prove helpful. Keep in mind that interviewing is a form of interpersonal communication. This means that the situation is not one-sided, but rather one in which two or more people interact through a question and answer format. Be prepared for both.

What You Should Do

* Do arrive on the scene well groomed.
* Do arrive on time - remember...early looks good.
* Do know something about the organization.
* Do come prepared with copies of important documents such as your resume, transcripts, letters of recommendation, citations.
* Do act positively. Try to show your enthusiasm for the job, and emphasize those qualities about yourself that show your strengths.
* Do shake hands with the interviewer.
* Do establish and maintain eye contact.
* Do answer questions clearly.
* Do be tactful and polite.
* Be prepared to ask questions of your own.
* Do end the interview with some expression of appreciation for the interviewers time.
* Do send a thank you note after the interview.

What You Should Not Do

* You should not use negative body language. Don't glance around, bite your nails, crack your knuckles, or play with your hair.
* Don't tell jokes. You might not be as funny as your friends have told you.
* Don't comment negatively about anyone- particularly previous employers.
* Don't bring anyone with you. You're all grown up now, so leave the crowd in the car.
* Don't arrive late. In the job market, this is not fashionable.
* Don't drop names. It is pompous, and may sound phony.
* Don't smoke, eat, or chew gum.
* Don't give yourself a time limit. Make certain that any other appointments you may have made are a few hours apart.
* Try not to be nervous - remember, the person who is interviewing you understands the difficulty of the situation. Remember that they were once where you are now.

Above All - Believe in yourself. Believe that if you are prepared, and know the rules of the game, you will eventually get what you want. Believe that you are as good and worthy as the next person.

Chapter 11

Large Group Dynamics
"Am I An Effective Communicator?"

A large group is one that is defined as having twelve or more participants. These participants are gathered together for professional concerns. Each member unites in order to communicate ideas regarding issues within current events, and issues dealing with individual concerns. These are usually questions on rights, freedoms, responsibilities, laws, organizations, managements, programs, professionalism, print and non-print media, and the assessment of all these concerns.

Assessment is a skill requiring the members within the group to critically examine the issue at hand. Each person within the group must be prepared to establish the merit, significance, and value of their chosen topic. As an example: Let us assume that the group has come together to discuss the formation of a new Teacher Education Program. Before any agreements or disagreements begin; before the bickering and "taking sides" start, there has to be a consensus as to whether or not there is any merit to its formation. The problem with most large groups is that there are so many people, and so many ideas floating around, that sticking to specific points becomes difficult. It is therefore crucial that the group succeed in integrating (putting together) their facts, and understanding the target points.

Evaluation of the issues - This process gives value to the information given between the group members. Based on their logical and rational findings, the group has now succeeded in integrating all the facts as a basis for a clear understanding of the issues at hand. In other words, now that the group knows there is an issue to discuss, they can begin to evaluate its importance.

In order to fully understand the function of a large group, we should briefly experience what this type of group discussion would be like.

1. Situate yourselves in a large circle so that each member of the group is able to see everyone else.
2. Each member of the group will be asked to discuss, assess, and evaluate the most important aspect of human behavior - specifically; communication.
3. Place - in ranking order - the skills that are used most often during interpersonal communication using the statements listed below:

   * The communication behavior that impresses/pleases me the most in others.
   * What I have learned from others.
   * What I am knowledgeable in - what I've learned.
   * The communication behavior that most displeases or discourages me about others.
   * What I expect of others.
   * How others appear to me.
   * What are my intentions with regard to the other people I am dealing with.
   * How do I go about interpreting what others do.

Once you have designated a number (1-8) to each of the statements above, you should be prepared to analyze the following questions: 1. Were you at all frustrated that the members of the group might not have agreed with your particular assessment? (Keep in mind that even though there are only eight statements, the chance of total agreement between all group members is very slight). 2. Did you cope with the disagreement in a "mature" fashion, or did you find yourself withdrawing and paying little , if no attention to what was going on in the group? 3. Did you find yourself feeling any degree of hostility towards the other members of the group because they did not agree with you, or did you find that you really didn't care enough to feel much of anything? 4. Did you distinguish the statements made between the people - who said what - or did it all seem like a blur where you were uncertain (or uncaring) as to what was said? 5. Did you find that there were many misunderstandings between the people in the group? 6. Was the session at all valuable for you, or did you find that it was a waste of your time? 7. Did you get enough opportunities to discuss your particular opinions? 8. Are you able to effectively explain some of the nonverbal cues that you received from the other group members in terms of their support or non-support of your beliefs? 9. Did you ultimately agree with the outcome of the discussion?

Large Group Techniques - The process of a large group discussion is a complex one. It is hard enough dealing with two or three people at a time because there are always differences of opinion, but the chances of working out an amicable solution is still quite a bit easier in this situation. With a little patience, each person will get the opportunity to air his/her feelings and beliefs, and a solution can be arrived at painlessly. In the large group discussion, where a dozen (or more) people are involved, there are many factors to contend with. The following points are important to remember:

1. Each member of the group *must* be totally involved in the effort to achieve a particular goal. Unlike the small group where each individual stands out clearly and prominently, it is easy to get lost within the large group. Don't allow yourself to fade away into the crowd; be alert at all times, and willing to participate - that's what the group effort is all about. Each person working collectively as a unit will ultimately make the group a success.

2. Remember that people have a tendency to analyze who the person is rather than what it is that they are saying, and this could lead to potential problems within the group. It's important to realize that personalities should never be the issue within the structure of a successful group effort.

3. Remind yourself to listen critically to what others are saying. The stronger you feel about a particular issue, the more you will probably have to say about it - and the less you will want to pay attention to others. Keep in mind that just because you may talk more than anyone else, it does not necessarily mean that you are right, or that others will agree with your thoughts. Sometimes, the best thing to do is to listen carefully to what everyone has to say, and then use their ideas (or pieces of them) to express your own theories. A wonderful way of getting people's attention is to use their name while expressing an idea of your own. An example of this would be: "John just said something very interesting, and for the most part, I agree with him...the part I don't agree with however is..." By using John's name, you can be fairly certain that he will listen to you, as well as anyone else who happened to agree with what he was originally saying. The point here is that listening to others can actually help to get your own ideas across.

4. Remember that regardless of who you are dealing with in a group, each person has their own views. Your best friend in the whole wide world does not necessarily feel the same way you do about everything. Although it is true that you usually choose many of your friends based on your similarities to each other, there are always differences. It is the rare group of friends that agree on every issue.The difference here is that with friends, you are more willing to accept their beliefs because you care for them, and are therefore more sensitive to their feelings.

5. A checklist should be devised to keep group pressure at a minimum. At any point where the group seems to be at a standstill - where no work is being accomplished, or hostilities are high - getting back on track with a vote, or consensus, will alleviate some of the tension, and hopefully promote movement towards an inevitable conclusion.

6. Don't allow yourself to become apathetic (uncaring). As we discussed in the chapter on Listening, find some aspect of what is going on in the group to hold your interest - particularly, "what's in this for me?". That should be your "hook;" establishing in your own mind what the importance the discussion has to your life. In other words, don't tune out .

7. Keep in mind that similar to a newspaper reporter, the information you give - particularly what you are stating as a "fact"- must be supported. Make sure you are able to verify any statements you make based on quotations, statistics, testimonials, or facts.

8. Be sincere in your effort to achieve the goals of the group. Be honest with others, and with yourself. The ultimate success or failure of the group depends on each and every person involved.

Possible Discussion Topics

Rights

The use of experimental drugs should be allowed in prisons as long as they are done solely on people who have been given life sentences.

Freedoms

Both evolution and the theory of creation should be taught in the public schools.

Responsibilities

Welfare checks should be abolished, and the government (or other existing agencies) should be held both accountable and responsible for finding work for those people who are unemployed.

Laws

The drinking age should be raised to 23, since records indicate that most accidents occurring due to drunk driving happen to people under this age.

Organizations

Professional athletes are paid too much money for the actual service they perform.

Management

The United States should definitely continue its efforts towards involvement in world affairs.

Programs

Despite all the negative publicity, television serves a worthwhile purpose for children.

Professionalism

Winning is everything.

In terms of the large group, consider the following questions:

1. What was the most important media event within the past month, and how was it covered?
2. Which form of media provides the consumer with the most objective perspective?
3. Does the media distort the truth? If so, in what way? Which form of media is the worst culprit?

Bibliography

Avery, Elizabeth, Jane Dorsey and Vera Sickels. *First Principles of Speech Training.* Englewood Cliffs, New Jersey: Prentice-Hall, 1928.

Bianchi, Doris Balin, Wayne Bond, Gerald Kandel and Ann Seidler. *Easily Understood.* Wayne, New Jersey: Avery Publishing, 1981.

Fisher, Hilda. *Improving Voice and Articulation.* ☐Boston: Houghton Mifflin, 1975.

Floyd, James. *Listening: A Practical Approach.* Glen View, Ill.: Scott Foresman, 1982.

Makay, John J. *Public Speaking - Theory into Practice.* Florida: Harcourt Brace Jovanovich, Inc., 1992.

Mayer, Lyle V. *Voice and Diction.* 7th edition. Dubuque, Iowa: Brown, 1985.

Sarnoff, Dorothy. *Make the Most of Your Best.* New York: Holt, Rinehart Winston, 1970.

Sarnoff, Dorothy. *Speech Can Change Your Life.* New York: Dell Publishing Co., 1970.

Seidler, Ann, Bianchi, Doris Balin. *Voice and Diction Fitness: A Comprehensive Approach.* New York: Harper and Row, 1988.

Trager, George. *Language and Languages.* New York: Intext, 1972.

Verderber, Rudolph. *Communicate.* California: Wadsworth Pub. Co., 1990.

CPSIA information can be obtained at www.ICGtesting.com
Printed in the USA
BVOW03s0449070115

382116BV00006B/64/P

9 780761 803607